CW0*********

Innovating Organization and M

The search for competitive advantage serves as the ... organizational strategy. This book highlights four key points in the analysis of competitive advantage and financial success that have not been given the attention they deserve: First, that organizational design and management processes may be strategic resources in their own right; second, that organizational design and management processes can be deployed to create new strategic resources; third, that managers have begun to think of organizational design and management processes in a proactive way rather than seeing them more passively as necessary facilitators of success; and, fourth, that this new way of looking at organization and management requires a search for new ways of structuring organizational design and managerial processes. These points are driven home through case studies of the Danish firms LEGO Group, Vestas Wind Systems, Coloplast, Chr. Hansen, IC Companys, and NKT Flexibles.

NICOLAI J. FOSS is Professor of Organization and Strategy at the Copenhagen Business School and Professor of Knowledge-based Value Creation at the Norwegian School of Economics.

TORBEN PEDERSEN is Professor of International Business at the Department of Strategic Management and Globalization at the Copenhagen Business School.

JACOB PYNDT works for Nordea, a leading Nordic-based pan-European bank, where he is involved with business strategy issues with a primary focus on the outsourcing of functions and processes.

MAJKEN SCHULTZ is Professor at the Department of Organization at the Copenhagen Business School, International Research Fellow at the Centre for Corporate Reputation, Saïd Business School, University of Oxford, and senior advisor to the Reputation Institute.

Innovating Organization and Management

New Sources of Competitive Advantage

NICOLAI J. FOSS
Department of Strategic Management and Globalization
Copenhagen Business School
Department of Strategy and Management
Norwegian School of Economics

TORBEN PEDERSEN
Department of Strategic Management and Globalization
Copenhagen Business School

JACOB PYNDT
Nordea Bank Danmark A/S

MAJKEN SCHULTZ
Department of Organization
Copenhagen Business School

CAMBRIDGE
UNIVERSITY PRESS

CAMBRIDGE UNIVERSITY PRESS
Cambridge, New York, Melbourne, Madrid, Cape Town,
Singapore, São Paulo, Delhi, Tokyo, Mexico City

Cambridge University Press
The Edinburgh Building, Cambridge CB2 8RU, UK

Published in the United States of America by Cambridge University Press,
New York

www.cambridge.org
Information on this title: www.cambridge.org/9781107648227

First published 2012

Printed in the United Kingdom at the University Press, Cambridge

A catalogue record for this publication is available from the British Library

Library of Congress Cataloguing in Publication data
Innovating organization and management : new sources of competitive advantage /
Nicolai J. Foss... [et al.].
    p.   cm.
ISBN 978-1-107-01105-2 (hardback)
1. Organizational effectiveness.   2. Strategic planning.   3. Management.
4. Success in business.   I. Foss, Nicolai J., 1964–
HD58.9.I56   2011
658.4′063–dc23
                                                                2011025057

ISBN 978-1-107-01105-2 Hardback
ISBN 978-1-107-64822-7 Paperback

Contents

v

Figures

Tables

Boxes

I New sources of competitive advantage

Why are some firms successful – perhaps continually – while others are not? This is *the* fundamental question in the field of strategic management. In this regard, we argue that more attention needs to be dedicated to the role of organizational design and management processes in an attempt to understand corporate success. In this chapter, we provide an overview of our main arguments and explain a number of the key concepts and ideas used throughout this book.

The search for corporate success serves as the basis for organizational strategy. In the jargon of the strategic management field, the search for success is equivalent to the search for competitive advantage – the potential to earn above-average returns. The key question, then, is the following: What are the sources of those competitive advantages?

The answers provided by almost fifty years of academic research and practitioner interest have varied widely. Early research stressed that a strategist's aim should be to ensure that the various functions of the firm are tightly integrated and aligned with the firm's external environment. Later work, the most notable of which is the well-known five forces framework developed by Michael Porter, put almost all of the emphasis on how the strategist handles the environment in terms of positioning the firm relative to the threats posed by various competitive forces.[1] The internal workings of the firm have been the subject of less interest, although Porter himself later added an analysis

---

[1] The five forces framework is covered in virtually all strategy textbooks. The original source is Michael Porter's 1980 book, *Competitive Strategy* (New York: The Free Press).

of value creation in firms through his notion of the value chain, which can be broken down into activities and value drivers.[2]

In recent decades, the business "environment" in its broadest sense has been radically reshaped. Globalization and its related process of deregulation mean that traditional bases of firm advantages, such as privileged or unique access to financial capital, labor, land, or markets, have declined in importance. In their place, a firm's ability to build, hone, upgrade, leverage, and extend specialized productive knowledge – so-called "capabilities" or "competencies" – is increasingly viewed as important, particularly those "dynamic capabilities" that allow a firm to modify its existing routines, procedures, or capabilities (Chapter 2 provides a primer on these ideas).

Our message in this book, therefore, is that there are sources of competitive advantage and financial success that, while never entirely absent from strategic management, have not been given the attention they deserve. These sources of competitive advantage are rooted in organizational design and management processes.

For example, consider a group of firms that includes DuPont, General Motors, Sears Roebuck, 3M, Toyota, Lincoln Electric, and Oticon. Even if you do not know that Lincoln Electric is a world leader in the production of arc welders or that the Danish hearing-aid producer Oticon plays a similar role in the hearing aid industry, you would be able to deduce that there is a high degree of diversity in this group of firms. Their industries, sizes, and organizational forms differ considerably. However, there is one striking similarity: A substantial part of the success of these firms can be ascribed to the ways in which they have structured their organization and management processes.

In the 1920s, DuPont, GM, and other major American corporations implemented an organizational structure known as the "multi-divisional form" (the M-form). On the basis of this organizational

---

[2] The value chain is now recognized as a staple of strategic management. The original source is Michael Porter's 1985 book, *Competitive Advantage* (New York: The Free Press).

BOX 1.1 **The M-form**

"Multidivisional form" (M-form) describes a type of organizational structure that consists of a set of semi-autonomous units, typically product divisions, which are mainly controlled by the financial targets set by corporate headquarters. This organizational form substantially reduces the monitoring burden placed on the headquarters. The M-form combines complementary activities (R&D, production, sales, etc.) in organizational units. The relative autonomy available to units in an M-form organization creates room for local experimentation and flexibility.

The M-form of organization is typically depicted in contrast with the U-form (unitary), which was common prior to the introduction of the M-form. The U-form pools similar tasks in organizational units. Therefore, instead of defining divisions on product criteria, they are defined on the basis of task criteria. This organizational format is harder to manage but may offer scale advantages.

The classical work on these organizational forms is *Strategy and Structure: Chapters in the History of the American Industrial Enterprise* by Harvard University Business History Professor Alfred Chandler (Cambridge, MA: MIT Press). The book, published in 1962, revolutionized the field of business history.

concept, major industrial firms were organized in divisions defined by products rather than by function (see Box 1.1).

This organizational redesign offered several benefits. First, it reduced the coordination challenges faced by corporate headquarters and released managerial attention, which could be refocused on corporate strategy issues. Second, it made it easier to define performance targets for divisional managers and reward them accordingly.

In 1991, Oticon implemented a new version of the M-form in the form of a highly decentralized "spaghetti organization" – a radical attempt to build an internal market for projects and jobs inside the firm. Bottom-up initiatives were stimulated by delegating the rights to initiate and run major research and development (R&D) and

---

BOX 1.2 **The Oticon spaghetti organization**

The turnaround in Oticon, a world leader in the hearing aid industry, is a common topic in organizational change literature. To restore innovativeness and entrepreneurial spirit in a firm that had become a low performer in the industry, CEO Lars Kolind decided to adopt an organizational form that was designed to mimic the market with respect to creativity and flexibility.

The "spaghetti organization" – named for its ability to be simultaneously both flexible and structured, like cooked spaghetti – was implemented on August 8, 1991 at 8:00 a.m. It consisted of a very flat structure with considerable autonomy allotted to employees to start and participate in development and marketing projects. The adoption of this organizational style restored entrepreneurial spirit in the company and produced a series of breakthrough innovations that led to impressive financial performance.

The story of Oticon is told in Nicolai J. Foss's "Selective intervention and internal hybrids: Interpreting and learning from the rise and decline of the Oticon spaghetti organization," *Organization Science*, 14 (2003), 331–49.

---

development projects to employees. This was complemented with an emphasis on high-powered performance incentives.

Oticon was not the only company to adopt radically new concepts in organization. In the 1980s, 3M was one of the first firms to refine the role of the firm as an incubator and financier of spin-offs. Toyota's experience with quality circle organization goes back to the 1950s and lean production has similar origins. Many contemporary management principles, such as discounted cash flow and activity-based costing, were developed, at least partly, as management practices in functioning companies.

MANAGEMENT INNOVATION

A significant amount of evidence suggests that the new organizational arrangements were vital to the performance successes of the firms that

BOX 1.3 **Management innovation**

Julian Birkinshaw, Gary Hamel, and Michael Mol have recently drawn attention to "management innovations." In an award-winning article entitled "Management innovation" (*Academy of Management Review*, 33 (2008), 825–45) and in various other books and articles, they argue that academics and practitioners alike have emphasized innovations in products and processes but have paid much less attention to management innovations. They explicitly cite the examples mentioned above (the M-form and the spaghetti organization) as examples of management innovations.

Birkinshaw and Mol's *Giant Steps in Management: Innovations that Change the Way You Work* (London: Prentice Hall, 2007) identifies what the authors argue are the fifty most important management innovations of the last 150 years.

implemented them. However, these arrangements greatly contributed not only to the performance successes of the relevant firms but also to the *novelty* of these situations. At the time of their implementation, the M-form, the spaghetti organization, the 3M incubator model, and the Toyota quality circles were highly *innovative* organizational practices. They may therefore be regarded as distinct "management innovations," on a par with innovations in products and production processes.

Little is known about the conditions that prompt management innovations and the effects that arise from such innovations. Managers who seek to innovate processes and organizations therefore have little decision support in management research.

One reason why we know relatively little about management innovations is that – in their pure form – they are quite rare. It is sometimes argued that an innovation is something that is entirely new, such as the invention or adoption of a new production process. Such innovations occur more frequently in products or production processes than in management practices and organizational design.

However, from a realist perspective, newness comes in degrees. A change in organizational design or management processes can be new to the world, to an industry, to a firm, or to a manager. While such a novelty may not be entirely new in a global sense, it may still be a source of advantage. A firm in an industry may benefit from imitating organizational forms, management practices, or business models used in other industries. In fact, new organizational designs and management processes tend to spread following their introduction to an industry by a pioneer firm (often inspired by developments in other industries). Industry incumbents later imitate the pioneer. This was true for the spread of the M-form, although it took that particular organizational form several decades to cross the Atlantic from the USA to Europe.

If we wish to understand how new organizational designs and management processes may give rise to successful performance, we cannot limit ourselves to those management innovations that are innovations in the strict, new-to-the-world sense. The perhaps more mundane management innovations – those innovations that are new to an industry or even "only" new to a firm – are certainly also interesting and relevant. This is the perspective we take in this book.

ORGANIZATIONAL DESIGN AND MANAGEMENT PROCESSES: SOURCES OF COMPETITIVE ADVANTAGE

The dominant thinking in strategic management stresses the importance of assets, such as reputation, intellectual property rights, and relations with suppliers and customers. Less attention has been dedicated to organizational design and new management processes. However, the above discussion highlights the fact that such designs and processes can serve as *strategic resources* for firms.[3] In other words, if they are properly organized and deployed, such resources

---

[3] In some cases, this was only realized *ex post*. For example, in General Motors, the M-form appears to have been implemented as a last-ditch effort to save a firm that was close to bankruptcy. The amount of rational planning and foresight behind the implementation seems to have been miniscule. However, the new organizational form contributed to the success of the firm.

can contribute decisively to corporate success. Thus, they contribute to the value the company can create and the value it can appropriate. They also help to make sure that the focal firm's level of appropriated value is higher than that of the competition.

As mentioned above, management academics have only recently begun to put their academic talents to use in the analysis of management innovation. Therefore, the ways in which management innovations and improvements in organization and management processes can contribute to competitive advantage are far from fully understood. Despite cases such as those discussed here, the role of organizational design and management processes as drivers of value creation, value appropriation, and the competitive advantages of firms is still neglected by practitioners and management academics alike. It is not unfair to say that there is still a strong tendency to think of these designs and processes as necessary facilitators of successful performance rather than as drivers of such performance in their own right, although this may be a somewhat crude generalization.

THE PURPOSE OF THIS BOOK

Four key ideas

The key purpose of this book is to improve management students' and academics' appreciation of the importance of organizational design and managerial processes to a firm's success. We emphasize both theoretical arguments (in this and the following chapter as well as in the concluding chapter) and case descriptions.

We develop four key points theoretically and illustrate them empirically. First, we argue that organizational design and management processes may be strategic resources *in their own right*. In other words, innovation in organization and management may create value, may assist in the appropriation of value, and may sustain these processes on levels above those attained by the competition.

Second, organizational design and management processes can be deployed to *create new strategic resources*. Notably, organizations

---

BOX I.4 **Key ideas**

Organizational design and management processes:

1. can serve as strategic resources;
2. may be deployed to assist in the creation of new strategic resources;
3. are increasingly considered by managers in a proactive way; and
4. may sometimes be described as "management innovations."

---

can be designed to increase their receptivity to outside knowledge and ideas.

Third, managers have begun to think of organizational design and management processes in a *proactive* way rather than seeing them more passively as necessary facilitators of success. This is evident in a number of our cases. The interest in business models that began with the dot-com revolution, and its related focus on the stark contrast between the companies of the "old economy" and those of the "new economy," most likely did much to stimulate this interest.

Fourth, this new way of looking at organization and management requires a search for *new* ways of structuring organizational design and managerial processes. In this regard, we establish a link with the management innovation theme (see Box 1.3).

Our cases and their lessons

To drive home these points, we examine a series of business cases encompassing the Danish firms LEGO Group, Vestas Wind Systems, Coloplast, Chr. Hansen, IC Companys, and NKT Flexibles. These companies differ significantly across a number of basic dimensions, such as industry, size, and age. However, these firms all explicitly treat their organization and management systems as key strategic resources. Moreover, they view their organization and management processes as more than just passive facilitators of strategies. The philosophy that underlies the experimentation with organization and management processes in these firms is that there is more to organizational design than just the implementation of efficient ways of organizing those resources that the firm already controls. In fact, these firms *explicitly* see organizational design and management processes as structures that can further the development of those resources that will allow them to compete in the future. In other words, they think of their organizational and management processes as what the strategic management literature defines as "dynamic capabilities."

A fundamental difference between the case examples discussed in this book and the cases mentioned above (DuPont, Sears Roebuck, etc.) is the role of organizational design and management processes in the strategy of the firms in question. For the Danish firms investigated here, organization and processes do more than support the firm's strategy – they are, in a very real sense, *part* of the strategy. This may sound similar to the idea of a business model – the way in which a company makes money in terms of articulating competencies to a specific environment through a defined mission. However, we have more in mind than this well-established concept.

Consider the toy producer LEGO Group, the eighth-largest firm in the global toy industry and one of the world's most recognized brands. In recent years, LEGO® has engaged in a major turnaround program – a crucial component of which is a series of deep-seated changes in the firm's organizational and management processes. Notably, the firm's current organizational design goes beyond supporting the firm's overall strategy: *The design itself and its complementary management processes are viewed as sources of new learning for the organization.* Such new learning, in turn, may give rise to new capabilities that can serve as the foundation for new strategies.

In particular, LEGO has adopted an organization form designed to improve its ability to tap into the creativity of LEGO fans and consumers. It has done so through such initiatives as the LEGO Community (which organizes hardcore fans and lead users, some of whom have become LEGO Certified Professionals) and by supporting

> BOX 1.5 **Open innovation**
>
> The basic idea behind "open innovation" is that companies increasingly need to source the knowledge needed in their innovation process from external knowledge sources. In other words, they cannot rely solely on knowledge produced internally, such as knowledge produced through the R&D function, if they wish to remain competitive. They increasingly need to tap into knowledge held by suppliers, customers, academics, and firms that control complementary technologies.
>
> An excellent introduction to open innovation can be found in Henry Chesbrough's *Open Innovation: The New Imperative for Creating and Profiting from Technology* (Boston: Harvard Business School Press, 2003), which coined the concept of open innovation.

user communities created by fans, including user-organized conventions. This has led to a continual process of what the company refers to as "co-creation by fans." In fact, LEGO is moving beyond the user-innovation model and is, in general, striving to make its corporate boundaries more permeable. This shift includes moves toward closer cooperation with suppliers, as declared by CEO Jørgen Vig Knudstorp:

> We are in the process of breaking up the value chain and inviting people in everywhere in the value chain. This is a paradigmatic shift that has huge implications for management, for our mindset, for incentive structures, for creativity and for all other aspects of the firm.

In effect, LEGO has adopted an "open innovation" model – shifting much of the creation and sourcing of knowledge from internal sources to external sources – and has taken it to what seems to be an extreme.

This example illustrates that organization and management processes can serve as sources of competitive advantage and success not only because they are resources in their own right but also because they contribute to the creation of new strategic resources. This is not the way practitioners, gurus, and management academics have typically thought about organization.[4] Traditionally, organization and management processes have been about organizing resources that are already controlled by the firm or at least accessed by it. From this perspective, the aims have been to deploy and link these resources more efficiently and to extract more and better services from them. The first issue concerns coordination, while the second concerns motivation.

However, organization also plays a role in fostering the learning, exploration, and innovation that leads to new strategic resources. The introduction of such a perspective implies a shift in focus from the firm's given portfolio of resources to the need for dynamic capabilities that allow an organization to adopt, develop, and maintain organizational designs and management processes that will provide it with a competitive edge. This is the view we seek to present, explore, and illustrate in these pages.

The research behind this book

We wrote this book on the basis of a conviction that too little practically relevant research exists on a topic that seems vital to an increasing number of companies: How to change, update, rejuvenate, and innovate organizational design and management processes so that they become more than simple facilitators of strategies. In our view, these elements can serve as important strategic resources in their own right. We approach this phenomenon in an explorative and inductive manner. In other words, we study concrete cases in detail rather than relying on secondary or statistical information.

Work on this project commenced in the fall of 2007. At that time, the project group (i.e., the authors of this book) defined the main research

---

[4] Two important exceptions are presented by the management gurus Tom Peters and Gary Hamel, who have long championed the idea that companies need to design their organization and management processes to allow for ongoing idea creation. See, for example, Tom Peters's *Liberation Management* (New York: Ballantine Books, 1992) and Gary Hamel's *The Future of Management* (with Bill Green; Boston: Harvard Business School Press, 2007).

questions and decided on the sample selection criterion – Danish firms from different industries that actively used novel organizational designs to gain competitive advantages. On the basis of this criterion, six case firms were selected. A series of semi-structured interviews was then carried out in the case firms in the spring and early summer of 2008. At least two members of the project group were present at every interview. Although a basic interview protocol was used, interviews were generally open-ended. The interviews were all transcribed and the cases were then written based on the information gathered during the interviews, as well as data from annual reports, newspaper articles, and other publicly available sources. All of the cases were sent to the case companies for fact checking.

The goal of the interviews was to move closer to an understanding of the ways in which organizational designs are deployed to assist firms in their attempts to gain competitive advantage and financial success. Therefore, we chose firms in which some basic dimensions of organizational and management innovation could be inductively derived from their experiences (see Chapter 9 for a discussion of these dimensions). We also wished to illuminate the ways in which organizational and management innovation might interact with elements such as organizational culture. More generally, we wished to be able to identify likely facilitators and stumbling blocks for these processes.

Although we kept these dimensions open when selecting the case firms, notions of radical organization and management innovations were implicitly present in the selection of the firms. Innovations ranged from the deep-seated organizational overhaul of the LEGO Group to the more modest changes seen in Chr. Hansen. However, we made no *a priori* decisions regarding more specific issues, such as the complementarity of organizational elements, or the relation between formal aspects of organization and "softer" elements, such as cultural factors.

Despite this precaution, our design still has elements of "sampling on the dependent variable." We have chosen firms that have, thus far, been relatively successful with the organizational and management innovations they have implemented. Furthermore, the firms originate from the same homogenous national environment. We spoke with senior managers who were sympathetic to or enthusiastic about the organization and management innovations, and who were often the driving forces behind those innovations. Therefore, biases are an obvious danger in both the case descriptions and our concluding interpretations.

However, our aim is not to use the empirical material to prove that such innovations lead to improved performance (although we hypothesize that this is, in fact, the case). The cases are primarily intended as illustrations and, secondarily, as vehicles for generating hypotheses about those changes in management and organization that are so radical that they border on innovation, and how such innovations may improve performance. Specifically, the cases in this book illustrate several key ideas by suggesting that:

- managers increasingly view changes in organizational structures, mechanisms, and processes as distinct sources of appropriable value creation;
- managers increasingly recognize that changes that are so radical that they amount to organizational and management innovations are important sources of competitive advantage;
- globalization is a potent driver of the ongoing process of experimentation with organizational forms and management processes; and
- organizational and management innovations take many forms and differ along multiple dimensions.

The rest of this book

In the next chapter, we discuss some of the ideas introduced in this chapter in more detail. We present a brief primer on some of the central concepts in contemporary strategic management and show how our theme of changes in organizational design and management processes tie in with these ideas. We then move on to our six cases, which explore different aspects of changes in organizational design and management processes. For example, the LEGO Group case places considerable emphasis on LEGO's attempts to make its corporate boundaries more permeable. The Coloplast case highlights that company's approach to organizing the process of innovation, while the IC Companys case considers a modern approach to M-form organization. Taken together, the cases help to illuminate important aspects of those changes in organizational design and management processes that are imperative in modern business conditions. Our concluding chapter presents a discussion of lessons to be learned from the various cases.

2 Causes of firm success: From resources to organization and management

INTRODUCTION

Given our concern with the ways in which organization and management contribute to corporate success, we find ourselves squarely in the universe of strategic management. Fundamentally, strategic management is about coordinating activities related to the delivery of value to customers in a way that is not only supportive of success but also different from the competition – perhaps even unique. In fact, the former (success) is largely derived from the latter (differentiation). While strategists and strategic management academics may agree on this basic view, there are numerous paths to differentiation and success may be assessed in a variety of ways. In this chapter, therefore, we briefly survey some of the key ideas on superior firm performance, heterogeneity, and strategic management that have emerged in recent decades.

Specifically, we discuss a range of perspectives on how resources and capabilities contribute to competitive advantage, and argue that such ideas need to focus more on understanding the interplay between resources and capabilities on the one hand and organization and management on the other. We show that: (1) The organizational design and management processes of a firm may be a distinct resource for that firm; and that (2) improvements and changes in these factors may contribute to sustaining competitive advantages; not least because (3) they may assist in the process of building new strategic resources and capabilities.

FIRM RESOURCES AND CORPORATE SUCCESS

Causes of differential corporate performance

The core goal of strategic management research is to investigate why some firms are successful while others are not. In other words, it seeks out those factors that result in above-normal financial returns, typically over an extended period. Armed with the identification of those factors, strategic management academics offer advice and teaching that may later become manifest in strategic practice.

In this regard, more than four decades of research into strategic management has allowed scholars to identify a range of different sources of competitive advantage and superior financial performance. In their search for sources of competitive advantage, researchers have traditionally concentrated on such factors as whether the firm is positioned in an attractive industry or whether it controls certain strategic resources. Indeed, the latter is, by far, the dominant focus in contemporary strategic management research. Strategic resources may include superior production capabilities, patents, star employees, superior human resource management (HRM) systems, super brands, and the specific, highly effective ways in which seemingly mundane activities "click" in a firm. In fact, the list is seemingly endless.

Why do such resources matter? Fundamentally, resources differ in their capacities to create value for customers, lower costs or appropriate value. Brand names differ across firms with respect to the first capacity, production facilities differ with respect to the second, and contractual relations differ with respect to the third.

Resources determine the product market strategies that firms can adopt and the value these strategies contribute, while also influencing the value firms can appropriate from deploying certain strategies in product markets. While presumably all or virtually all strategies may be imitated, imitation can only be achieved at a cost. Thus, specific products may be reverse-engineered, often at a modest cost. However, reverse-engineering of a product is not equivalent to producing it at competitive cost. Similarly, the product may only sell

---

BOX 2.1   **The resource-based view**

The view of strategy presented here is associated with the resource-based view (RBV). The RBV was developed by strategy theorists in the 1980s, although it originated some time earlier. Professor Jay B. Barney of Fisher College at Ohio State University is a key RBV proponent. Barney's main contribution is a paper entitled "Firm resources and sustained competitive advantage" (*Journal of Management*, 17 (1991), 99–120). In this paper, he develops the VRIN framework – the insight that resources must be Valuable, Rare, In-imitable, and Non-substitutable if they are to contribute to sustained competitive advantage.

Barney is also the author of several textbooks that present the RBV, including *Gaining and Sustaining Competitive Advantage* (Boston, MA: Addison-Wesley, 2007).

Ideas on core competencies, capabilities, and dynamic capabilities are closely related to the RBV. It may be argued that they focus on particular types of resources.

---

well under a specific brand name. These simple observations highlight the important role of the resources underlying product market strategies: Successful, defensible product market strategies are those that are underpinned by resources that are not only able to contribute decisively to value creation and appropriation but are also difficult to access through imitation. By definition, therefore, such resources must be scarce and must be prohibitively costly to imitate.

Characteristics of resources

To sort among entries on the long list of potential strategic resources, researchers have developed criteria that resources must meet in order to qualify as strategic resources. Such resources have the potential to yield a sustained competitive advantage. One of the most well-known lists of such criteria is attributed to strategy professor Jay B. Barney. According to Barney, in order to offer sustained competitive advantage, resources must be *valuable*. This may be broadly understood as a requirement that the resource must enable the firm to exploit an opportunity or neutralize a threat in the environment. More concretely, valuable resources are those that allow the firm to offer products at low cost or to offer products for which customers are willing to pay a premium. In other words, they make the firm capable of creating value.

However, if valuable resources are in abundant supply, other firms will quickly acquire such resources and implement them in strategies that are identical to those of the successful firm (in the process, the prices of the resources are likely to be bid up as well). Thus, the value creation arising from the resources will quickly be eroded to the break-even level. To counteract this effect, resources must also be *rare* – only possessed by the focal firm or very few competing firms.

Even if resources are both valuable and rare, they may still be imitable. In essence, imitability is closely tied to costs, so in order to qualify as a strategic resource, a resource must be valuable, rare, and (very) *costly to imitate* – it should be prohibitively expensive for the competition to build similar resources. A final condition is that the resource should be (very) *costly to substitute*. In other words, it must be prohibitively expensive to implement similar strategies by using other (substitute) resources.

When all of these criteria are met simultaneously, a resource may serve as the foundation for a competitive advantage. Taken together, these criteria form a useful checklist for a strategic audit: Any single resource controlled by a firm can be evaluated using the above criteria. For example, while resources such as cash or generic machine tools may add value, they are unlikely to be rare. While a resource such as a custom-made machine tool may be both valuable and rare (at least in the short run), it may not be terribly difficult to imitate (reverse-engineer).

"Holy Grail" resources

Therefore, the search is on for those resources that are valuable, rare, *and* costly to imitate and substitute – the "Holy Grail" of superior performance. Strategic management scholars have argued that resources that have arisen through historical processes unique to the individual firm, that are socially complex, and that embody "tacit" knowledge (i.e., knowledge that is costly to articulate) are those resources that are most likely to meet these criteria.[1]

The case firms in this book exemplify these ideas in various ways. For example, one of LEGO's key resources is its brand, which buyers view as an effective signal of creative, quality toys. The same is true for the famed LEGO brick. Well aware that imitating a plastic brick is not an extremely complex undertaking, LEGO invests substantial resources in legal protection that can maintain the barriers to imitation around the brick. However, a recent court decision in the EU means that LEGO cannot enjoy protection of the brick as a three-dimensional EU trademark (see http://tiny.cc/ea63o). Therefore, LEGO will have to focus on other means of protection against imitation. For LEGO, non-imitable factors might include the complexity of its productive operations and its management practices.

The Coloplast case illustrates the importance of a set of socially complex resources that are the result of a specific historical process. Notably, Coloplast's user-driven product development and design capabilities have evolved through a complicated, path-dependent historical process that dates back more than five decades and has involved innumerable specific pieces of knowledge, communication exchanges, and cycles of trial and error. Much of this has become embedded in the interaction, organization, management systems, culture, and values of Coloplast. As a result of this important historical legacy, Coloplast's product development and design capabilities may be costly to imitate.

---

[1] For this reason, later extensions of the RBV have emphasized resources such as "competencies," "capabilities," and "dynamic capabilities" (Barney, "Firm resources and sustained competitive advantage"; I. Dierickx and K. Cool, "Asset stock accumulation and sustainability of competitive advantage," *Management Science*, 35(12) (1989), 1504–11; D. Teece, G. Pisano, and A. Shuen, "Dynamic capabilities and strategic management," *Strategic Management Journal*, 18(7) (1997), 509–33).

WHY THE ORGANIZATION AND MANAGEMENT OF RESOURCES MATTER

Fitting organization and management into the RBV

The RBV is arguably the dominant view in contemporary strategic management teaching. Our experience confirms that it is also highly influential and widely used in practice. Although we have few problems with this analysis, in our view it does not go sufficiently far. One main concern is that the RBV does not clarify the role of organization and management processes.

Concepts such as "capabilities" or "competencies" certainly refer to organizational processes but they also refer to plenty of other issues. A firm, for example, can have a superior competence in a given business area because it controls dedicated production machinery that is operated by particularly skilled employees who work in a knowledge-sharing environment under management that is appreciative of individual efforts in the direct production activities and in terms of taking on extra roles, such as assisting colleagues. Removal of one of these elements may mean that the competence will disappear. Therefore, a competence may arise from a complex interplay among physical, human, and organizational resources.

Indeed, we often use words like "competencies" and "capabilities" to refer to the results of this interplay. However, from a practical management point of view, these terms are not necessarily helpful. Managers want to know how to build and modify capabilities. This requires specificity about what exactly constitutes, for example, a capability, how it is built and so on. Thus, for managers it may be more helpful to focus on organizational design and management processes, and on how these affect concrete resources. These processes are often relatively easier to change in the short run than the often ill-understood capabilities and competences. However, we are by no means claiming that changing organizational structures or fundamentally redesigning reward systems is a simple or easy task.

BOX 2.2   **Organizational design and management processes**

We use "organizational design" mainly to refer to the choice of organizational structure and roles (i.e., departmentalization, specialization, specification of interdependencies between units, etc.), as well as the specification of metrics and rewards, and the matching of talent and roles. In other words, organizational design defines the structure and boundaries of a firm's business processes.

We use "management processes" to refer to management's planning, controlling, coordinating, etc., functions.

Amy Kates and Jay R. Galbraith's *Designing Your Organization: Using the Star Model to Solve Five Critical Design Challenges* (San Francisco: Jossey-Bass, 2007) presents a detailed insight into organizational design based on Galbraith's work.

Organizing resources

In order to better understand how resources and capabilities are embedded in and interact with organizational design and management processes, we must move beyond the idea that firms are bundles of resources and capabilities. Although resources and capabilities are *stocks* that may yield a *flow* of services, such services do not appear automatically and they are not automatically deployed to production. Rather, they have to be called forth and the diverse services from diverse resources have to be coordinated. Thus, employees may have to be motivated and incentivized; tasks have to be defined to determine which services are needed and when; the internal division of labor (services) has to be determined; standard operating procedures must be defined so that the different services mesh; authority has to be allocated across the organization to make optimal use of management services, etc.

To call forth services and to coordinate and deploy them across various activities is the purpose of a firm's organizational design and its management processes. This somewhat static purpose is traditionally seen as the main purpose of organization and management, but, as we explain later, the *upgrading* of a firm's portfolio of resources and capabilities, and the services they can yield, is also orchestrated through the firm's organizational design and management processes. However, let us consider for a moment how the issues of organizing and deploying resources and capabilities, and the resulting services, enter into the understanding of differential corporate performance:

- *Are resources efficiently organized?* Does the firm have human resource management policies and practices in place that help human resources to contribute to organizational value creation? Does it have the right management information systems? Does it have reward systems that are appropriate for the kind of activities in which the firm is engaged? Are existing contracts with stakeholders, such as suppliers, customers, and employees, the best possible ones?

- *Is the organizational design superior to that of the competition?* The organizational design and management processes should lead to employees and other resources supplying those services that, when deployed in such activities as production, marketing or R&D, result in a level of appropriable value creation that exceeds that of the competition. This calls attention to whether the internal division of labor is the most appropriate. Have tasks been combined so that production processes can be carried out smoothly? Are tasks allocated to the right units? Do organizational units communicate in an efficient manner? Is authority over decisions allocated to the right managerial positions?

- *Can the competition emulate the firm's organizational design and management processes?* If competitors can, over time, imitate the design and processes that provide the firm with an advantage, that advantage is not sustainable. Thus, although the design and the processes may give rise to a high level of value creation, the firm cannot hope to appropriate much of the created value unless the design and processes are difficult to imitate. Sometimes the organizational designs and management processes of firms are the result of a complex process of incremental improvement over time, as in the case of Lincoln Electric (see below). That process may be very difficult to replicate. At other times, the organizational design may have appeared virtually overnight, as in the case of Oticon, but that design may be very difficult for the competition to imitate because it is so radical and requires a set of supporting cultural beliefs.

- *Does the firm explicitly seek to improve its organizational design and management processes?* Within the framework outlined thus far, one way to maintain a competitive edge is to continue to upgrade – or, more radically, change – organizational design and management processes. For example, an advantage may be maintained by continuously striving to improve management information systems or by fine-tuning reward systems. An advantage may also be maintained, or built anew, by radically changing the organization and/or its management processes.

A complex and uncertain cultural process

Gaining and maintaining performance success from organizational design and management processes is a process often characterized by extreme complexity and significant uncertainty. For example, the Danish toy producer LEGO has undergone a series of largely complementary and reinforcing organizational changes. These were, however, not implemented in a "big bang" manner. Rather, they were introduced incrementally, perhaps because a solution in which multiple organizational components were changed simultaneously would overwhelm the organization with complexity. A more incremental, experimental approach in which smaller changes in the organizational design would be tested was adopted instead. However, from the perspective of those employees, managers, and stakeholders that have been part of these changes, there has been nothing "incremental" about them. For example, one of the first initiatives implemented by CEO Jørgen Vig Knudstorp was to increase the number of plastics suppliers from one to a handful. This seemingly small change in a sourcing arrangement was perceived internally as a significant change with strong cultural overtones.[2]

---

[2] Jørgen Vig Knudstorp, inaugural speech as Adjunct Professor, Copenhagen Business School, September 5, 2008.

This suggests that cultural factors – including institutional-ized belief systems that pertain to the nature of the organization, its role and justification, and its typical ways of acting relative to employees and other stakeholders – are part and parcel of organiza-tional change processes. Thus, changes in organizational design and in management processes can be constrained by strongly held val-ues and beliefs that may influence (constrain or enable) the ability to maneuver. Certain things cannot be done in a firm because of the constraining force of corporate culture. However, while culture can inhibit change, it can also facilitate it. Successful change manage-ment requires an understanding of this dual and potentially contra-dictory role.

Given the importance of cultural factors in organizational change processes, attempts to influence values and beliefs are often explicitly incorporated as part of the design exercise. Nearly all of the case firms included in this book stress the importance of culture in the process of redefining their organization. The process of influencing organizational values and beliefs is even more complex and uncertain than trying to influence the more tangible levers of organizational design and management processes. However, this only makes it more important to understand the role of values and beliefs in processes of organizational change, and in the innovation of managerial and organ-izational practices. In fact, one of the key themes emerging from this book is the *strongly interconnected relation* that exists between the tangible and less tangible aspects of an organization in processes of implementing change, and innovating design and management processes.

Advantages arising from organizational design and management processes

The ways in which firms can establish and maintain (long-lasting) advantages by means of their organizational design and their manage-ment processes are still poorly understood. This claim may surprise some. Management academics have written extensively about organizational change and restructuring, and about corporate renewal. Furthermore, much attention has been devoted to such concepts as total quality management, business process re-engineering, and six sigma, and to the potential contribution of such practices to overall corporate performance. Indeed, many management scholars have high-lighted the role of organization in influencing competitive advantage.[3] However, there are a number of differences between existing research on the link between organizational design and management processes and the arguments presented in this book.

Most of what has been written on the ways in which the design of organization and management processes may contribute to corporate performance is *partial* in the sense that it focuses on *single* organiza-tional practices. For example, scholars examine the contribution of particular types of management information systems, reward schemes, cost allocation practices, or HRM systems to competitive advantages and financial performance. This is a partial view in the sense that it is focused on the performance effects of a single element of the overall organizational design.

Practices such as total quality management (TQM) or business process re-engineering imply more thorough organizational changes. For example, the implementation of TQM may bring drastic changes in the autonomy possessed by shop-floor employees, while business process re-engineering may bring about drastic changes in organiza-tional structure. However, such organizational changes do not capture the kind of changes in organizational design and management pro-cesses that we are concerned with in this book. Instead, we focus on changes that:

• *reflect an explicit strategic focus* in that they are expected to significantly contribute to organizational value creation;

---

[3] It is, perhaps, indicative that Barney renamed the "VRIN" framework of his 1991 article "VRIO" in his later textbook (see Box 2.1). In the latter term, "O" stands for "organization."

BOX 2.3 **Specific organizational practices and performance**

Many studies exist in management literature about the ways in which individual organizational practices can influence overall organizational performance.

For example, David. B. Balkin and Louis R. Gomez-Meija examine how rewards matter for performance and how this depends on the environment in which the company is positioned. ("Towards a contingency theory of compensation strategy," *Strategic Management Journal*, 8 (1985), 169–82). H. M. Beheshti considers activity-based costing as a driver of corporate performance in "Gaining and sustaining competitive advantage with activity based cost management systems" (*Industrial Management and Data Systems*, 104 (2004), 377–83).

Francisco Mata, William. L. Fuerst, and Jay B. Barney discuss the contribution of IT to competitive advantage ("Information technology and sustained competitive advantage: A resource-based analysis," *MIS Quarterly* (1995), 487–505) and conclude that only IT skills (rather than code and hardware) can give rise to sustained competitive advantages. Mark Youndt, Scott Snell, James W. Dean, and David P. Lepak ("Human resource management, manufacturing strategy, and firm performance," *Academy of Management Journal*, 39 (1996), 836–63) show that human resource management practices may affect corporate performance but that this depends on the overall strategy of the company.

- are made not just to organize a given set of resources and capabilities but also to contribute to the *building of new resources and capabilities*; and
- are *overarching* in the sense that they involve changes in a number of different aspects of organizational design and management processes (e.g., changes in structure, information systems, and reward systems) and not just one or two. In other words, they fundamentally change the configuration of organizational elements.

In the following section, we describe a view of organizations that can support the understanding of such changes. As this description is relatively abstract, readers who are less interested in theory can skip the section and jump directly to the section entitled "Organizational and management innovation."

ORGANIZATIONAL DESIGN AND MANAGEMENT PROCESSES: THE CREATION OF APPROPRIABLE VALUE

To better understand our arguments concerning organizational design and management processes as potential sources of value creation and appropriation (and, potentially, of sustained competitive advantage), it is useful to systematically consider the following questions: 1) Why do organizational design and management processes matter in the creation of value in the first place? 2) Under which circumstances might the created value be appropriable? 3) How can a high level of appropriable value creation be sustained?

It is, of course, possible to argue that a particular organizational design or management practice that adds "value" is "rare" and "costly to imitate" (see Barney, "Firm resources and sustained competitive advantage"). However, as we wish to know *why* this is the case, we must look at organizations in somewhat abstract terms and adopt a more detailed view of what organizations are.

Conceptualizations of organizations

The way we think about organizations depends on what we want to explain. In strategic management research, it has become customary to think of organizations as "bundles of resources." As explained earlier, we need to supplement this view with an understanding of how resources are embedded in organizational and managerial structures and processes, as our emphasis is on these structures and processes, and how they help create appropriable value and, perhaps, competitive advantages.

Organization design theory traditionally argues that organizations consist of certain elements that are common to all organizations. According to this view, organizations differ because the elements are combined in different ways. Henry Mintzberg's 1980 book *Structures in Five: Designing Effective Organizations* (Upper Saddle River, NJ: Prentice Hall) offers a particularly well-known version of this view. Mintzberg synthesizes a massive amount of research on organizational designs into four clusters of organizational elements[4] that yield the famous five configurations: Simple Structure, Machine Bureaucracy, Professional Bureaucracy, Divisionalized Form, and Adhocracy.

Such macro-views of organizations are extremely helpful in many ways. However, a somewhat more *detailed* view is sometimes necessary if we are to understand the inner workings of organizations and the reasons why changes and innovations in organizational and management may have implications for appropriable value creation and competitive advantage. Therefore, these macro-views of organizations have been refined by the economic approach to organizations.

Organizations as structures of rights

A detailed view of organizations may begin with the common view that organizations first and foremost consist of organizational members. Such organizational members have individual goals, preferences, expectations, and motivations, and they are engaged in the joint effort of reaching organizational goals. The extent of this engagement depends on how the organization is set up in terms of such factors as

---

[4] Mintzberg summarizes these in the following manner: The "(1) five basic parts of the organization-the operating core, strategic apex, middle line, technostructure, and support staff; (2) five basic mechanisms of coordination-mutual adjustment, direct supervision, and the standardization of work processes, outputs, and skills; (3) the design parameters-job specialization, behavior formalization, training and indoctrination, unit grouping, unit size, action planning and performance control systems, liaison devices such as integrating managers, teams, task forces, and matrix structure, vertical decentralization (delegation to line managers), and horizontal decentralization (power sharing by nonmanagers); and (4) the contingency factors-age and size, technical system, environment, and power" (Henry Mintzberg, "Structure in 5'S: A synthesis of the research on organization design," *Management Science*, 26(3) (1980), 322–41, p. 322).

BOX 2.4   **The economic approach to organizations**

The economic approach to organizations applies economics tools to the analysis of organizations, especially in terms of their inner workings and their mutual relations.

Pioneered by Nobel Prize winners Ronald Coase, Herbert A. Simon, and Oliver E. Williamson, the economics of organizations has become a large, fertile field that is highly influential in management research and is taught at many business schools. The economics of organization includes transaction cost economics, principal agent (or "agency") theory and ideas on property rights.

Highly accessible introductions can be found in J. A. Brickley, C. W. Smith, and J. L. Zimmerman's *Managerial Economics & Organizational Architecture* (New York: McGraw-Hill, 2008) and in Paul Milgrom and John Roberts's *Economics, Organization, and Management* (Upper Saddle River, NJ: Prentice Hall, 1992).

The rights perspective developed here draws from these sources. A particularly succinct statement of the idea can be found in James S. Coleman's "The design of organizations and the right to act" (*Sociological Forum*, 8(4) (1993), 527).

---

the division of labor and motivational mechanisms. Basically, all organization theory starts with this idea.

However, this starting point can be refined by noting that organizational members hold *decision rights* over the use of corporate resources. Here, a "right" simply indicates that someone (perhaps the company's owners or a manager) has conferred authority on an organizational member to make use of company resources within a decision domain. He or she may possess that right exclusively or he or she may share it with other organizational members. Therefore, an R&D manager may make decisions within a specified budget without consulting a higher-ranking manager, but it is understood that he or she cannot use available resources for purely private purposes or in ways that harm the company. When entering a company, organizational members also acquire rights to income – the right to be remunerated on the basis of the value that the organization creates. Therefore, despite the somewhat legalistic terminology, rights can be thought of quite concretely. The term refers to the "authority" that organizational members hold over corporate resources and the remuneration that they are entitled to receive in exchange for their efforts.

We can relate these ideas to examples of management innovations. In the Toyota lean system, for example, shop-floor employees hold the formal right to halt the production process if they detect a quality problem. TQM provides the right to undertake joint decision making in cross-functional teams. The essence of the Oticon "spaghetti organization" is that it delegates the rights to initiate and run development and marketing projects, rights that were previously held by top and middle managers, to employees at lower levels. The M-form delegates extensive decision rights to divisional managers and controls them by designating divisions as profit centers. The organizational innovation for which Lincoln Electric is famous is the definition of performance measures for its employees.

Notably, changes in organizational design and management processes are often changes in the rights to decide over the use of resources as well as changes in income rights, as illustrated by the above examples. This provides a basic conceptualization that unifies the many otherwise different ways in which such designs and processes can change.

In organizations, rights to make decisions over corporate resources are constrained in a number of ways. Standard operating procedures, job descriptions, and organizational charts provide formal delineations of rights – they specify who has the right to use specific corporate resources, when they can use them, and where they can be used. Corporate policies and value statements also help to define rights. For example, a firm may deprive its employees of the right to make use of social networking sites, such as Facebook, during working hours. However, the definition and allocation of rights to use corporate resources have significant informal elements. Indeed, in any given organization, members hold views (that may not always be mutually consistent) about their own rights and entitlements, and about the rights and entitlements of other organizational members. In fact, these views form an important part of organizational belief systems.

The views held in an organization about such rights and entitlements are an integral part of organizational culture. Organizational cultures provide delineations of rights by informing employees (as well as outsiders) of "how we do things here." In a broad sense, reward systems, including bonuses, wage structures, and promotion procedures, constitute income rights. In this regard, management information systems convey the information that allows for the monitoring of employee (or organizational unit) performance, which is a prerequisite for the functioning of reward systems.

In this view of organizations, the organizational design and the design of management processes are matters of getting the rights allocation correct. Traditionally, organizational design theory has focused on structuring rights so that specialization advantages are realized and activities are coordinated. This has implications for such aspects as departmentalization, the design of standard operating procedures, and job designs. More recently, organizational scholars (particularly those with an economics background) have considered how income rights should be structured. For example, they have analyzed which employees should be included in bonus schemes, how large the incentives should be, and how incentives should differ depending on the number and kind of tasks the employees undertake.

Why rights matter: Value creation and appropriation

Rights matter because they determine what organizational members can do with specific corporate assets and how they are remunerated. In other words, rights matter because they define the *opportunities* that organizational members face (with whom can one interact? Where? When? What can be done with corporate resources?) and because they provide incentives (i.e., income rights), which influence the *motivation* of organizational members. They may also influence the motivation of organizational members to improve their *abilities* in any number of ways, such as by engaging in training. In turn, motivation, opportunities, and ability give rise to employee action. The aggregate of such action is what we (really) mean when we talk about firm activities, such as pursuing certain strategies or entering markets.

Intuitively, the way in which rights are structured has an effect on organizational outcomes, especially in terms of organization-level value creation. It matters whether job descriptions and standard operating procedures lead to the reasonable coordination of activities within and between organizational units (departments and divisions). In terms of employee effort, whether employees are offered bonuses or flat wage rates also makes a difference, although these particular relationships are moderated by such elements as organizational culture and management style. The extent to which employees will specialize relative to the firm (that is, show "loyalty") depends on their sharing in the surplus generated by the firm – their income rights. In other words, the amount of value that organizational members expect to appropriate influences the effort they will contribute to the firm and the investments they will make in that regard.

In sum, the kind and amount of services that an organization can extract from the resources that it can access depend upon the allocation of organizational rights. These services are proximate causes of organizational value creation. Therefore, organizational value creation is dependent on organizational rights allocation.

In the static view favored by economists, the problem of allocating rights is a matter of choosing a mix of rights that leads to the maximization of organizational value creation over an appropriately defined time horizon. Such allocations are subject to a number of constraints, which are not discussed here.[5]

---

[5] This view is at the core of contemporary debates on shareholder versus stakeholder models: Does one model or another maximize organizational value creation? This illustrates the generality of this view.

BOX 2.5   **LEGO CEO Jørgen Vig Knudstorp on decision rights**

When discussing the recent turnaround in LEGO, Knudstorp explicitly told the authors of this book: "In the final analysis, it is all about decision rights – who has the right to do what, at which time, how, where, etc., with LEGO's corporate assets? Thinking about it in this way is one way of linking day-to-day management issues with the longer-term goals of value creation" (interview, May 6, 2008).

Of course, the basic idea that it is possible to design organization and management processes in a value-maximizing manner is a theoretical abstraction. In the real world, which is fraught with uncertainty and less than perfectly rational managers and decision makers, this view, in its pure form, is unrealistic. However, it is possible that managers make explicit attempts to design organization and management processes in a value-maximizing manner and that the heuristics they employ in this undertaking are close to the theoretical reasoning we present here (see Box 2.5).

Sustaining the creation and appropriation of value

Suppose a firm has introduced an organizational design and a set of supporting management processes that result in a level of value creation that exceeds that of the competition. The opportunity costs incurred by organizational members are easily covered. The owners of capital receive a return that exceeds the returns they would receive in alternative employments of their capital. Organizational members and capital owners would obviously prefer that this situation continue, but will it?

As discussed earlier, the answer to this question depends on whether the relevant organizational design and management arrangements are *imitable*. Intuitively, one may expect that they are, indeed,

---

BOX 2.6 **Lincoln Electric**

Founded in 1895 in Cleveland, Ohio as a producer of arc welding equipment, Lincoln Electric represents the essence of sustained financial success. The company has consistently realized positive (and often huge) economic returns in every year of its existence. It is currently a Fortune 1000 company and has sustained its position as the dominant firm in the arc welding technology industry (despite intense competition).

The company first came to the attention of management professors with the publication of Fast and Berg's case *The Lincoln Electric Company* (Harvard Business School Case, 1975). Paul Milgrom and John Roberts argue that the cause of Lincoln's success lies primarily in the ways in which the elements of its sophisticated reward system interact ("Complementarities and fit: Strategy, structure, and organizational change in manufacturing," *Journal of Accounting and Economics*, 19 (1995), 179–208). Joseph A. Maciariello's *Lasting Value: Lessons from a Century of Agility at Lincoln Electric* (New York: Wiley, 1999) contains a detailed investigation of Lincoln's development.

---

easily imitable. However, this is not necessarily so, as illustrated by the case of Lincoln Electric (see Box 2.6).

Many researchers convincingly argue that Lincoln's sustained success can be attributed to its consistent application of high-powered incentive systems (i.e., income rights that are closely linked to employee results), as well as the organizational arrangements it has implemented to support these systems. Under the management of James F. Lincoln (the brother of founder John C. Lincoln) Lincoln Electric adopted piecework schemes and an Employee Advisory Board in 1914. It implemented employee stock ownership as well as an employee suggestion program in 1925. In 1935, it introduced incentive bonuses. Throughout its history, the company has continuously sought to improve its performance pay programs by fine-tuning and extending its bonus systems.

The result has been impressive financial performance on the organizational level with returns on stockholder equity twice as high as the average in the metals industry. This, in turn, has allowed production workers to earn salaries that are double the industry average. The basis for these high wages is, of course, high labor productivity, which may not only be a result of the high-powered performance incentives but also of the willingness on the part of employees to commit to the firm in terms of specializing their human capital. The result is employees that work smarter, harder, and in a more coordinated manner.

This performance is one that many firms wish to replicate. One book about Lincoln Electric is advertised in the following way: "This book shows you how to duplicate these pioneering ideas and follow the brilliance of the Lincoln management system. The results of this system include happier customers, more prosperous workers, and richly rewarded shareholders."[6] Indeed, Lincoln Electric does not appear to do things that cannot, *in principle*, be done by other firms. The Lincoln Electric model is largely public knowledge: The firm has been a case-teaching favorite for decades (Fast and Berg, *The Lincoln Electric Company*) and its organizational arrangements have been heavily discussed in the business press. However, the fact is that Lincoln is *not* being imitated – the Lincoln experience remains unique. As far as we know, no other firm (either in the metals industry or in comparable industries) has adopted anything like its radical HRM policies. The question is: Why?

There are no easy answers to this question. However, we suspect that the likely reasons relate to the apparently high degree of alignment among the many aspects of the Lincoln organization in the production of favorable outcomes and the sheer complexity of this. Thus, the more organizational elements that are intertwined and the more complicated the relations among them are – the higher the complexity – the more difficult it is for would-be imitators to actually

---

[6] This is the book by Joseph Maciariello mentioned in Box 2.6. The quote is from the US branch of Amazon.com (accessed September 22, 2008).

emulate the organizational setup.[7] Moreover, Lincoln Electric's formal organizational and HRM policies are supported by norms and beliefs that have developed over an extensive history. Such a history-dependent, complex organization may be impossible for competitors to faithfully replicate, except at a cost that they are unwilling to pay.

INNOVATING ORGANIZATION AND MANAGEMENT

Renewing organizational design and management processes

Few firms can rely on the luxury of having stumbled, early in their existence, on a superior organizational design and superior management processes that will offer superior financial performance for decades and that require maintenance rather than substantial renewal (Lincoln Electric may exemplify such a firm). Rather, firms frequently have to renew their administrative systems, change their organizational structures, experiment with their reward systems, and reconfigure their organizational designs in novel ways. In fact, firms are increasingly confronted with the need to renew these aspects of their organization because long-run viability depends on the fit between the organization and the environment. For their part, environments are changing faster, becoming more unpredictable, and making new demands on organizations and management.

Several megatrends are behind these environmental shifts. The most important is arguably the combined forces of liberalization and globalization, which have drastically changed the basic business models of many multinational companies. Whereas such firms used to employ business models that stressed the utilization of home-country-based advantages (superior production capabilities, marketing skills, etc.) in foreign markets and dictated the replication of value chains

---

[7] Such difficulties of imitation also apply to Lincoln itself. As former Lincoln CEO Donald Hastings recounts, the company had great difficulties in replicating its organizational design and managerial practices during its (ultimately ill-fated) international expansion in the 1990s ("Lincoln Electric's harsh lessons from international expansion," *Harvard Business Review*, May–June (1999), 163–72). However, the difficulties may have had more to do with resistance among European employees to the company's reward systems than with difficulties of replication.

across countries, multinationals today are increasingly breaking up their value chains and recognizing that strategic initiative can, in principle, emerge from anywhere in the value chain – not just from corporate headquarters. Such firms typically engage in substantial modifications of their organizational design to accommodate the new, more entrepreneurial business models. Advances in information and communications technologies support these processes, while considerations of legitimacy may reinforce them.

In the new competitive environments, organizations not only have to become more adept at matching the demands of the environment with the capabilities of the organization, they also have to continuously renew their resources and capabilities – and they have to develop capabilities for continuously handling such adaptations.

As we have argued, the firm's organizational design and management processes are key factors – and are being recognized as such – in the identification, sourcing, building, and exploitation of resources and capabilities. Therefore, the new role for organizational design and management processes is not only to fit the environment at a given point in time but, perhaps more importantly, to also enable the organization to source and build those resources and capabilities that will make the firm capable of engaging with the competition in the future.

Organizational and management innovation

As we pointed out in Chapter 1, firms sometimes change their organizational designs and management processes in ways that amount to *innovations* – that is, ways of doing things that are new to the firm, the industry, or the world. These innovations represent changes relative to current norms.[8]

---

[8] For practical purposes, "current norms" need to be defined. Are we talking about current norms for the firm, the industry, the nation, or the world? In the context of the cases in this book, we think of current norms on the industry level. The reason for this choice is that defining innovation relative to firm-specific current norms trivializes

Management innovations can be understood as new ways of increasing created value by coordinating activities and motivating stakeholders in novel ways. However, not all organizational and management innovations create value. Rearrangement of the organizational configuration does not guarantee success, regardless of how new the result may be. As is the case with technological innovations, 100 failed attempts may be necessary before a truly successful management innovation is created. However, compared to technological innovations, management innovations are typically more systemic in nature, and their implementation is more disruptive and costly for the organizations involved. Whereas companies can often experiment with and test technological innovations on a small scale, partial adoption or testing of management innovations is rarely feasible. Therefore, it is even more important for an organization to gain a better understanding of the characteristics of management innovations that create value and the conditions under which they can be successfully implemented.

Innovations related to the organizational design and management processes of companies amount to new ways of structuring decision and income rights. These include, but are not limited to, new ways of configuring and coordinating the internal division of labor, new ways of rewarding employees (i.e., income rights), new ways of allocating decision rights, new methods of measuring input and output performance, and new standard operating procedures.

Many different beneficial consequences may flow from such innovations, including reductions in the costs of coordination and motivation, lower production costs, and increased innovativeness. Even when innovations do not directly reduce costs or improve efficiency, they may be symbolically efficient. Thus, an organization that

organizational and management innovation – in this context, any organizational change becomes an innovation. On the other hand, thinking of current norms as relating to worldwide norms for organizing and managing is overly restrictive – under this criterion, few changes can qualify as truly innovative.

appears to be more innovative may find it easier to raise capital, serve customers, or attract prospective employees. Such benefits may translate into competitive advantages.

Building knowledge about organizational and management innovation

Despite the obvious importance of organizational and management innovation to firms, industries, and, perhaps, whole economies, research on this phenomenon is limited. In fact, as we explain in Chapter 1, explicit investigations into management innovation are a recent undertaking. As a result, relatively little is known about the phenomenon. For example, information about what initiates innovations in management processes and organizational design is scant. However, we are not entirely in the dark.

Business historian Alfred Chandler's classical account of the emergence of the M-form in four major US companies in *Strategy and Structure* offers one of the first speculative discussions of the causes of management innovation. His findings suggest that a sense of crisis spurred the invention of the multidivisional form in DuPont, Standard Oil of New Jersey, General Motors, and Sears Roebuck. Furthermore, he notes that the managers driving the innovation process in the respective companies were all relatively young and had not been in the positions they held at the time for very long. However, he does not claim any general validity for these findings.

In an article in *MIT Sloan Management Review*, Julian Birkinshaw and Michael Mol analyze eleven recent cases of management innovations ("How management innovation happens," *MIT Sloan Management Review*, 47 (2006), 81–8). They find that the invention of a new management practice, process, or structure is preceded by a combination of internal dissatisfaction with the status quo and inspiration from outside the company. Following invention, the innovation goes through a process of internal and external validation and, finally, the innovation may be diffused to other organizations.

More recent work by Mie Harder goes further than most studies with respect to documenting actual management innovation.[9] Harder uses a survey instrument targeted at approximately 1,000 of the largest Danish firms to clarify the incidence of management innovation and identify its antecedents. She finds that from 2006 to 2009, 25 percent of the 289 firms that responded implemented management innovations that were "new to the industry" and 63 percent engaged in management innovations that were "new to the firm." She also notes that manufacturing firms are more likely to engage in management innovation, that the desire to increase organizational efficiency is the main driver of the decision to engage in management innovation, and that management innovation is more common when firms are involved in other kinds of innovation as well.

In the following, we present six Danish "qualitative" cases that highlight deep-seated changes in organizational design and management processes, changes that are usually novel to the industry in question. They may therefore be seen as instances of management innovation.

[9] M. Harder, "Antecedents of management innovations," PhD thesis, Copenhagen Business School, 2011.

3 LEGO: Redefining the boundaries

In 2008, Jørgen Vig Knudstorp, CEO of the Danish toymaker LEGO, recalled the company's development during the preceding four years. According to Knudstorp, the journey had been a rollercoaster ride – overwhelming, uplifting, and, at times, bumpy, chaotic, and highly emotional. He joined the company's strategic business development unit in 2001 before becoming Head of Corporate Affairs and interim Chief Financial Officer (CFO) in 2003 (Figure 3.1). In 2004, he took on the Chief Executive Officer (CEO) position. At the time, the LEGO Group was suffering from annual losses amounting to billions of Danish kroner (DKK), which threatened the company's independence. The organization was stressed and its identity was unclear. The company had basically lost its way. The initial steps of Knudstorp's survival plan had been to regain financial control of the company and define its future direction.

From a financial perspective, the turnaround plan was successful. Following a 40 percent decline in sales, the LEGO Group reported annual losses of DKK 1.8 billion in 2004. However, in 2006 and 2007, net profits amounted to DKK 1.29 billion and DKK 1.02 billion, respectively (Table 3.1). Following the implementation of a number of cost-reduction initiatives – such as the relocation of production, the downscaling of the number of components used in production, the divestment of assets (including LEGOLAND theme parks), and a renewed focus on core product lines, user groups and markets – the LEGO Group had stabilized and was building a profitable business platform to serve as the backbone for sustainable growth in the years to come (Figure 3.2).

The turnaround did not only have a financial focus. The plan also inspired a more profound transformation process related to the innovation of the LEGO Group's business model in two critical dimensions. First, it marked a shift from a traditional "bricks and mortar"

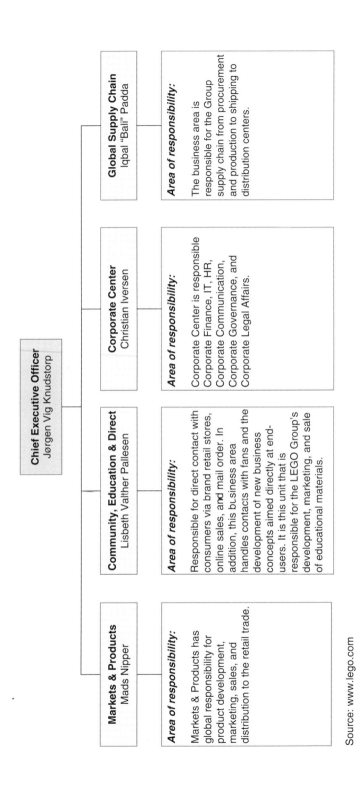

Chief Executive Officer
Jørgen Vig Knudstorp

Markets & Products
Mads Nipper

Area of responsibility:

Markets & Products has global responsibility for product development, marketing, sales, and distribution to the retail trade.

Community, Education & Direct
Lisbeth Valther Pallesen

Area of responsibility:

Responsible for direct contact with consumers via brand retail stores, online sales, and mail order. In addition, this business area handles contacts with fans and the development of new business concepts aimed directly at end-users. It is this unit that is responsible for the LEGO Group's development, marketing, and sale of educational materials.

Corporate Center
Christian Iversen

Area of responsibility:

Corporate Center is responsible Corporate Finance, IT, HR, Corporate Communication, Corporate Governance, and Corporate Legal Affairs.

Global Supply Chain
Iqbal "Bali" Padda

Area of responsibility:

The business area is responsible for the Group supply chain from procurement and production to shipping to distribution centers.

Source: www.lego.com

FIGURE 3.1 LEGO Group Organization

Table 3.1 *Financial highlights and key ratios*

	2008	2007	2006	2005	2004	2003
Income statement (DKK million)						
Revenue	9,526	8,027	7,798	7,027	6,295	6,770
Expenses	(7,522)	(6,556)	(6,393)	(6,605)	(6,394)	(7,919)
Operating profit before special items	2,004	1,471	1,405	423	(99)	(1,148)
Impairment of fixed assets	(–20)	24	270	86	(677)	(172)
Restructuring costs and other special items	116	(46)	(350)	(129)	(136)	(283)
Financial income and expenses	(248)	(35)	(44)	(51)	(75)	88
Profit before tax	1,852	1,414	1,281	329	(987)	(1,515)
Profit, continuing activities	1,352	1,028	1,290	214	(1,284)	(965)
Profit, discontinuing activities	–	–	–	–	(516)	77
Net profit for the year	1,352	1,028	1,290	214	(1,800)	(888)
Balance sheet (DKK million)						
Assets relating to continuing activities	6,496	6,009	6,907	7,058	5,160	8,785
Assets relating to discontinuing activities	–	–	–	–	1,638	–
Total assets	6,496	6,009	6,907	7,058	6,798	8,785
Equity	2,066	1,679	1,191	563	404	2,344
Liabilities relating to continuing activities	4,430	4,330	5,716	6,495	5,160	6,441

Table 3.1 (*cont.*)

	2008	2007	2006	2005	2004	2003
Liabilities relating to discontinuing activities	–	–	–	–	271	–
Cash flows and investments (DKK million)						
Cash flows from operating activities	1,954	1,033	1,157	587	720	989
Investment in property, plant and equipment	368	399	316	237	285	653
Cash flows from financing activities	–1,682	(467)	597	(656)	(70)	(205)
Total cash flows	128	592	1,925	1,570	443	(541)
Financial ratios (%)						
Gross margin	66.8	65	64.9	58	57.9	54.3
Operating margin (return on sales [ROS])	22.0	18.1	17.0	5.4	(14.5)	(23.7)
Net profit margin	14.2	12.8	16.5	3	(28.6)	(13.1)
Return on equity	72.2	71.6	147.1	44.2	(131)	(28.1)
Return on invested capital (ROIC) I	101.8	67.7	63.6	16.2	(2)	(13.5)
Return on invested capital (ROIC) II	113.8	77.1	67.4	15.2	(18.9)	(19.1)
Equity ratio	31.8	27.9	17.2	8	5.9	26.7
Equity ratio (including subordinated loan capital)	39.5	46.2	33.2	8	5.9	26.7
Employees						
Average number (full time), continuing activities	5.388	4.199	4.908	5.302	5.603	6.535

Table 3.1 (*cont.*)

	2008	2007	2006	2005	2004	2003
Average number (full time), discontinuing activities	–	–	–	1.322	1.029	1.160

Financial ratios have been calculated in accordance with the "Guidelines and Financial Ratios 2005" issued by the Danish Society of Financial Analysts. For definitions, please see the section on accounting policies. Financial highlights have been adjusted to reflect the LEGO A/S Group structure and are prepared in accordance with International Financial Reporting Standards (IFRS). Parentheses denote negative figures.

Source: LEGO Group Annual Report, 2007 and 2008

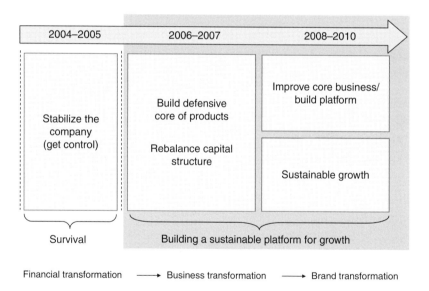

Source: LEGO Group Annual Report, 2007 and internal presentations

FIGURE 3.2 Strategy direction and phases

company and a philosophy characterized by vertically integrated value chain activities to a more network-oriented business model that entailed a looser vertical setup. Second, the LEGO Group's new business model made use of the "open source" concept – customers were increasingly invited to comment on products (prototypes), test them (LEGO City), co-develop them (LEGO Mindstorms), or even customize their own creations (LEGO Factory).

According to Knudstorp, as part of the company's changing business model these new aspects constituted a paradigm shift that had considerable implications for management, the company mindset and incentive structures in the LEGO Group. The Group's move toward a network-oriented company made boundaries permeable. One common concern was how the LEGO Group could empower and engage external stakeholders, including business partners, consumers, and society, while still attaching an appropriate value to the relationships.

Nearly all functional areas were involved, including product development and design, the supply chain, production, distribution, and marketing. Furthermore, most of the company's stakeholders were analyzed. Figure 3.3 pinpoints three key areas central to the company's changing business model.

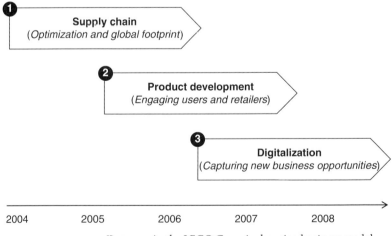

FIGURE 3.3 Key areas in the LEGO Group's changing business model

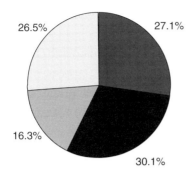

26.5%   27.1%

16.3%

30.1%

- Central and Southern Europe

- North America, Australia, New Zealand and United Kingdom

- Scandinavia, Benelux, Eastern Europe, Asia

- Community, Education and Direct

Source: LEGO Annual Report, 2007

FIGURE 3.4 Revenue split, 2007

TRANSFORMING THE COST BASE

As part of the turnaround plan, the LEGO Group had to optimize its cost base. This occurred in part through the relocation of production to low-cost areas. The Global Supply Chain division, headed by Executive Vice-President (EVP) Iqbal "Bali" Padda, was responsible for moving approximately 900 manufacturing jobs (out of 1,200) from Billund, Denmark to the Czech Republic and Mexico in order to realize DKK 1 billion in annual production cost savings. In addition, jobs were moved from Korea, Switzerland, and the USA to low-cost locations. Only the most complex production lines were kept in Billund (approximately 20 percent of total volume), which ensured that headquarters could preserve a certain competence and skill level, and keep in touch with various production steps, such as molding, processing and packaging. The LEGO Group had engaged Flextronics to operate production in the Czech Republic, Hungary, and Mexico. Given the size and complexity of the assignment, preliminary experiences with this arrangement were fairly positive. However, they also clearly demonstrated the challenges that face a company moving from vertical integration to a network constellation. How could the LEGO Group manage coordination and motivation issues and create the right levels of trust, culture, and standardization with its outsourcing partner Flextronics?

CUSTOMER INVOLVEMENT

A second factor in the Group's transformation was related to customer involvement in product development processes. Historically, the company had involved users in traditional focus group testing. Furthermore, as one of the front-runners in the toy industry, the LEGO Group was experienced in involving customers in the design and product development process to varying degrees through user testing, user co-development, and personal customization.

However, the situation in 2008 proved challenging for several reasons. First, the LEGO Group had essentially made use of unpaid manpower (typically the most hardcore fans) up to that point, which meant that it was relying on the insights of merely one percent of the customer base. Additionally, acceptance of the fact that users could come up with innovative, smart ideas required substantial buy-in, humility, and tolerance among the LEGO Group's product developers. Customer involvement could trigger organizational arrogance and opposition. Second, customer involvement had to be properly managed and controlled by the LEGO Group in order to shape ideas that would target the core users, namely children. User creations had to be aligned with the LEGO Group's product development guidelines to avoid any violations of the brand. For example, toys and landscapes inspired by modern war scenes were not acceptable under the brand's vision.

External inspiration helped ignite new product ideas inside the LEGO Group, but these ideas were often incremental in nature. Key concerns were therefore how the LEGO Group could:

1. establish the right framework and mechanisms to foster radical innovation;
2. take product ideas developed by adults and adjust them to fit children better; and
3. organize and involve children to a greater extent in the product development process.

Third, the company had to cope with the issue of intellectual property rights (IPR) and definitions of interfaces and roles when inviting customers. How could the company balance the engagement of enthusiastic users and user communities with the stakeholder surveillance apparatus and the need to have an appropriate juridical arsenal in place if IPRs were violated?

THE DIGITAL AGE

A third element of the LEGO Group's transformation involved digitalization. Breaking up the value chain presented the company with new business opportunities, which were facilitated by technological developments. LEGO products were initially made of wood. Later, LEGO molded bricks in high-quality plastic to ensure longevity. However, the company had not attempted to digitalize the original LEGO brick. As digital technology advanced, it wanted to explore business opportunities based on this kind of technology. Digitalization called for a fundamentally different type of communication with the market and customers. Traditional communication activities based on a physical distribution network were easier to control. Digitalization, in contrast, made the LEGO Group's communicative efforts subject to varying interpretations and was more difficult to monitor.

Another issue was how to create a true LEGO experience using digital technology. Would playing with digital LEGO bricks enable users to build extremely elaborate structures, foster creativity, and promote the same joy that came from building as when the bricks were physically present? In addition, this new business needed to be financially sustainable. In that respect, the open-source line of thinking, which is widely disseminated in the digital world, was a challenge. To what extent could the LEGO Group make its program codes available to external developers while still appropriating value and knowledge from digital activities?

In sum, the challenges related to the company's supply chain, product development, and digitalization made the organizational boundaries more permeable. The turnaround helped to establish a more sustainable, "future-proof" business platform that embraced business process optimization, while also creating room for innovativeness and creativity. Whether the LEGO Group could sustain its success depended on the company's ability to execute or, as Knudstorp stated, its way of "acting into new ways of thinking."[1]

AN INTRODUCTION TO THE LEGO GROUP

With the simple abbreviation of two Danish words – "leg" (play) and "godt" (well) – Ole Kirk Christiansen founded the LEGO Group in 1932 in a small carpenter's workshop. The company has since developed into a modern, global enterprise that is now the world's fifth-largest manufacturer of toys in terms of sales. Its products are sold in more than 130 countries. However, its headquarters remain where it all began – in Billund, Denmark.

Central to the LEGO Group's *raison d'être* are the concepts of "systematic creativity" and "lifelong play." In principle, the company's bricks stimulate and support a logical, disciplined approach to building or construction. At the same time, the nearly indefinite number of potential combinations highlights a creative, independent, and idea-based line of thinking. In fact, just six of the basic "eight stud" LEGO bricks can be combined in more than 900 million ways. When thousands of different brick designs and color combinations are added to the LEGO product range, the range of creative play possibilities effectively becomes infinite.[2]

Another key characteristic of LEGO relates to the bricks' durability and longevity, not only in terms of product quality but also in terms of customer segments spanning various age groups. While children constitute the company's core customer segment, LEGO products have gained an iconic status among adults who share the same passion for the extreme flexibility, simplicity, and creativity offered by the

---

[1] Presentation given at the Strategic Management Conference, Copenhagen Business School, December 12, 2006.

[2] www.designcouncil.org.uk/case-studies/lego/the-evolution-of-design-at-lego.

bricks. Still, children are the company's role models: "Children are inquisitive, creative and imaginative – with an innate urge to create. We must stimulate the child in each of us!" (www.lego.com). The same line of reasoning is included in the Group's mission, which is to inspire and develop the builders of tomorrow.

BOX 3.1 **Values and cultural heritage**

Throughout its history, the LEGO Group's strong values, at the organizational and brand level, have inspired decision making and have played a key role in the way business ideas are implemented. For example, the brand values – *creativity, quality, and fun* – are decisive for the Group's relationship with its users via a numerous groups and websites such as LEGO Factory or LEGO Club. During the 1990s, the Group extended and stretched the brand to embrace numerous product categories less related to the original LEGO idea of active fun and playful learning.

A key tenet of Knudstorp's turnaround and transformation plan involved a renewed emphasis on the core of the LEGO idea and thus broke with the idea that the LEGO brand could be applied or utilized sporadically. Knudstorp's niche strategy and plan signaled a return to the founder's motto *"only the best is good enough."*

The renewed focus with Knudstorp at the helm had important implications for organizational conduct and development. The handling of supplier relationships and the introduction of performance management serve to illustrate these ideas. Traditionally, the LEGO Group dealt with an exorbitant number of suppliers, roughly 11,000, as each engineer was allowed to form relationships with suppliers if he or she needed a specific material for a new product. This made it impossible for the LEGO Group's procurement staff to realize scale effects when they sourced materials. Thus, as part of the transformation process, the procurement organization was professionalized and given a strategic role. In some instances, the number of suppliers was reduced to gain greater economies of scale, and in others, new suppliers were introduced

BOX 3.1 (CONTINUED)

to encourage competition.[3] While financially rewarding, this move was regarded as a cultural revolution inside the company, according to the CEO.

Similarly, the introduction of performance pay heralded new times. The fact that the LEGO Group now explicitly distinguished between employees and honored high performers stood in sharp contrast to former principles of equality. Performance pay was a well-functioning management tool used to support and sharpen employees' focus on execution. The challenge was now to find the right balance between individual and team-based performance pay, a balance that could drive individual behavior as well as encourage internal cooperation.

Financial development

In 2003 and 2004, the LEGO Group reported a combined net loss of DKK 2.688 billion. The loss was primarily due to less successful business initiatives that had sought to stretch and apply the LEGO brand to relatively unrelated areas, such as television programs, software games, children's clothing, and accessories. A general lack of confidence in its core product, the LEGO brick, led the company to introduce new product lines and concepts that it hoped would be key growth drivers. The diversification strategy increased complexity, confused users and employees, and took the company away from its core. The poor financial results were further exacerbated by generally poor developments in the toy market and in key currencies.

The number of product components became symbolic of the LEGO Group's financial downfall as well as the financial survival plan. When the crisis was at its most severe, approximately 12,700 product components were used to make LEGO products. When the business transformation was nearly complete in 2007, the number of components had been reduced to roughly 6,000. Instead of blindly

[3] Keith Oliver et al., "Rebuilding Lego, brick by brick," *Strategy & Business*, August, 2007.

introducing new components, substantial efforts were made to reuse older components in new designs – a process that was not always gratifying for LEGO designers but benefitted the company's bottom line.

By addressing the carefree creativity among product developers, the LEGO Group actually reduced the complexity of product designs. This, combined with an increased focus on customer value and the adjustment of the cost base and assets to reflect lower revenues, allowed the Group to regain financial control in terms of positive bottom-line figures and rising operating margins. In 2008, the Group's sales amounted to DKK 9.5 billion, while net profits reached DKK 1.35 billion.

Products and markets

The LEGO Group's products fall into the following six categories. *Pre-school products*, such as LEGO DUPLO, consist of large brick elements that encourage children to build what comes into their minds. By the same token, *creative building* denotes standard LEGO sets where no instruction is needed other than the use of one's imagination. Via its *play theme* product lines, the Group added a further dimension to the joy of construction, namely that children can spend many hours playing with finished models. For instance, with LEGO BIONICLE, the company developed a complete story that combines construction toys and action figures. With *MINDSTORMS NXT*, LEGO users can design and program their own robot to perform various operations. *LEGO Education* targets the educational sector and has developed materials for both teachers and pupils. Lastly, LEGO has a number of *licensed products*, which are basically play themes based on movies, i.e., Star Wars and Indiana Jones, or books, for which the Group has acquired the rights (see the LEGO Group's profile brochure, www.lego.com).

From a product perspective, one of the LEGO Group's strategic mistakes during the 1990s was to aggressively expand its product portfolio and extend the brand. New products, such as software games, children's clothing, and accessories, were introduced with little focus on the core user groups and the company's *raison d'être*: Supporting creativity and problem solving skills. Brand extensions, combined with a fuzzy product philosophy, negatively affected the Group's culture and sparked internal conflicts, as new types of employees were hired to design new product lines and concepts. In addition, the vision and goals became unclear, as no united approach existed.

To reconnect the brand to its heritage, product lines were discontinued during the transformation. These included such toys as cars requiring little or no construction, as they did not live up to one of the company's most fundamental rules – toys must have a constructive element. In this respect, all LEGO products had to be highly constructible and deliver in terms of the joy of building or creating.

Future expectations

The size of the global toy market is decreasing and, in general, subject to a great deal of uncertainty. Nevertheless, the LEGO Group expects future organic growth of 3–7 percent per year and it aims to maintain high profit levels. The USA constitutes the company's most important single market and represented approximately one-third of retail sales in 2007 when combined with Australia, New Zealand and the UK. Scandinavia (including Eastern Europe) and Central and Southern Europe amounted to 26.5 percent and 27.1 percent of sales, respectively (see Figure 3.4). Many markets achieved double-digit growth in 2007, mainly driven by classic product lines like LEGO City, LEGO Creator, LEGO DUPLO, and LEGO Star Wars.

In the USA, the LEGO Group grew 12 percent in 2007, despite the fact that external analysts see the country as a diminishing toy market. For 2008, the company was expected to realize a 3 percent share (2.5 percent in 2007) of the market for traditional toys, enabled by the growing popularity of LEGO City, which was honored with the "Best Activity Toy of the Year" prize at the American International Toy Fair (*Børsen*, February 22, 2008). In light of its size alone, the US market was regarded as the main growth driver for the LEGO Group.

In addition, an unexploited potential existed for the company's core products in emerging markets.

Part of the company's growth ambitions involved a focus on and full exploitation of the potential in core products, coupled with launches of fundamentally new concepts inspired by the original LEGO idea of systematic play and creativity. In fact, 85 percent of the business is expected to still be based on core product lines in mature markets in 2015 (*Børsen*, July 21, 2008). Knudstorp's vision had a lot to do with sticking to the originality of the LEGO brand and being selective in terms of customer focus. The company aimed to satisfy and grow with those who love the LEGO brand, as opposed to convincing those on the periphery to buy.[4] The LEGO Group was to remain true to its original mission of producing toys that encouraged children to create and to use their imaginations.

SUPPLY CHAIN: OPTIMIZATION AND GLOBAL FOOTPRINT

As part of the turnaround, the LEGO Group embarked on a comprehensive strategy of right-sizing activities, the cost base, and assets. Critical elements of this strategy involved the optimization of supply links as well as the relocation of labor-intensive production. This, in turn, required a more global outlook. Prior to 2005, the Group had production and packaging facilities in Denmark, Switzerland, the Czech Republic, Korea, and the USA. For several years, the company had been producing at its factory in Kladno, the Czech Republic and using various sub-suppliers in China. In addition, production/packaging facilities in Korea served the Asian market, including Japan.

Given the scope of the crisis, the restructuring of the value chain was accelerated in 2005. Production facilities were closed in Denmark, Switzerland, and Korea and transferred to Kladno and to suppliers in Eastern Europe (LEGO Group Annual Report, 2005). Moreover, the LEGO Group's European distribution centers were centralized in

---

[4] Tyler Brûlé's interview with Jørgen Vig Knudstorp, available at www.monocle.com/ sections/business/Web-Articles/QA-with-the-CEO-of-Lego.

Table 3.2 *Production outsourcing overview*

Product category	Responsible	Location	Contract expiration
Technic	LEGO	Denmark	Not applicable
Bionicle	LEGO	Denmark	Not applicable
DUPLO	Flextronics	Hungary, China	2014
System	Flextronics	Czech Republic, Hungary, and Mexico	2014
Small Business	Sonoco	Poland	Not available

Eastern Europe. This, in combination with the relocation efforts, was expected to increase efficiency, improve servicing of the European market, and save costs. According to corporate management, the overriding goals were to restore the Group's competiveness and to ensure future profitability.

In 2006, as part of the shared vision strategy, the LEGO Group outsourced major parts of its production operations to Flextronics, a leading electronics manufacturing services (EMS) provider – a move that resonated well with the LEGO Group's asset-light business model that included offshoring production operations from Denmark to the Czech Republic and from the USA to Mexico (see Table 3.2). While LEGO System and DUPLO products were relocated to Flextronics's facilities in Eastern Europe, the production of technically more demanding products such as LEGO Technic and BIONICLE remained at the LEGO facilities in Billund. This setup allowed the LEGO headquarters to retain a number of critical competencies in molding, processing, and packaging. By the same token, the LEGO Group established a mechanical engineering unit and a production technology R&D unit next to its remaining production facilities in Billund. This was considered crucial to enhancing product development efforts.

In addition, Flextronics took over responsibility for the company's factory in Kladno in August 2006. The Group retained ownership of the buildings and plant equipment, while Flextronics was responsible for daily operations. Lastly, a number of packaging processes were transferred to the US packaging center and Sonoco's factory in Poland and to Greiner's factory in Slovakia.

Commenting on the Flextronics outsourcing agreement, Knudstorp stated:

> This is the last major step in our process of restructuring of the Group's supply chain, which has been implemented since 2004 with the purpose of cutting total production costs by 1 billion DKK. So far, we have yielded savings by closing our factories in Switzerland and Korea, enhancing efficiencies via the introduction of LEAN processes, upgrading our procurement processes and trimming product complexity. With the restructuring process, we want to improve our profitability while at the same time strengthening our competitive edge in an increasingly competitive market. (www.lego. com, press archive)

The LEGO Group's decision to use relocation and outsourcing as a means of restructuring its value chain was primarily motivated by cost structure and market proximity considerations. First, the Group out-sourced production to reduce costs, which enhanced its competitiveness and enabled a shift to more productive, higher value activities – namely innovation and product development. Specifically, the labor-intensive decorating, assembly, and packaging processes within product lines char-acterized by a high degree of uniformity and volume (like LEGO System products) were outsourced. Second, based on a thorough analysis of the company's supply chain, Mexico and the Czech Republic were selected as key hubs from which the company could serve the European and US markets. According to the Group, quality levels in a number of low-cost countries improved notably, while transport, communication, and trans-action costs related to operations in these countries decreased considerably (LEGO Annual Report, 2006).

The LEGO Group's relocation and outsourcing aspirations were grim reading for LEGO production employees. In total, 80 percent of the production would have been affected by the relocation process. In Billund, 900 out of 1,200 production jobs would be lost. Another 300 would lose their jobs as a consequence of the closure of the company's US packaging and distribution facility in Enfield, Connecticut. In addition, the Group's factory in Kladno, the Czech Republic, with approximately 600 employees, was taken over by Flextronics. Following the completion of the outsourcing process in 2010, the LEGO Group's headcount would be at approximately 3,000 compared to a total workforce of 8,300 at the end of 2003.[5]

Sourcing and relocation not a panacea

The LEGO Group's decision to outsource was not camouflaged. Pointing to the Group's critical need to adapt to globalization and benefit from it, the company communicated openly with employees. Management sought a dialog with regards to the challenges and possible solutions for affected workers. When the outsourcing plan was launched in June 2006, LEGO employees were instantly informed of the scope of the plan – that 75 percent of all LEGO jobs would be lost by 2010. Despite the obvious resentment and frustration among the staff, management was successful with this kind of frank, open communication, which established a sense of urgency to which most employees could relate.

While communication worked well during the outsourcing process, the LEGO Group encountered more serious challenges in globalizing its value chain in terms of process specifications and documentation, capacity utilization, effectiveness, and IT. On a cultural level, trust and misconceptions caused some friction. When

---

[5] In all fairness, the sizeable reduction in headcount was not strictly due to outsourcing processes. As part of establishing a new business platform (and an asset-light model), LEGOLAND Parks were divested, production facilities were closed in Switzerland, a general workforce alignment was undertaken, etc. (press release, June 20, 2006, www.lego.com). Globally, approximately 2,000 employees in production were to be affected by outsourcing.

sourcing on a global scale, the Group had to orchestrate product development activities in Denmark with volume manufacturing in the Czech Republic and Mexico, while also managing a tremendous flow of goods – approximately 21 billion brick elements flowed from production to retail stores annually. This called for strong internal coordination and sound partnerships, particularly with Flextronics. These partnerships had to be based on compatible systems and processes.

Outsourcing many years of accumulated experience in producing LEGO sets required extensive documentation and process specifications. Despite the substantial share of manual labor, knowledge was embedded in the minds of the operators and was not necessarily well-documented in manuals that would make the knowledge easy to understand and readily implemented. The fact that the LEGO production had taken place in-house was, to some extent, reflected in many implicit or unwritten rules and processes. In order to secure future product quality, such rules and processes were formulated and incorporated through certification and increased participation by the LEGO Group in sub-suppliers' production (LEGO Annual Report, 2006).

Another challenge related to IT systems. The LEGO Group had implemented SAP throughout the organization. Despite some teething troubles, the system now coordinated and planned production. However, Flextronics used BAAN as its production planning system, which was incapable of planning production of the elements essential to LEGO brick production. The fundamental idea of LEGO is that approximately 6,000–8,000 bricks apply to a broad range of LEGO models. These bricks must be combined in numerous ways and in numerous groups during the production process.[6]

Capacity utilization, uptime and effectiveness comprised other important challenges in the outsourcing process. The LEGO Group was used to running with almost 100 percent utilization of the capacity in its production processes, while other companies using molding machines

[6] Interview with CEO Jørgen Vig Knudstorp, March 11, 2008.

in their production processes ran at 70 percent utilization or lower. From an economical perspective, 70 percent utilization was unacceptable for the LEGO Group. During the spring of 2007, the outsourcing agreement was seriously tested – the Mexico site suffered from severe logistical problems while the Kladno site was understaffed, leading the Group to scale up production in Billund and postpone the dismissals announced in 2006 (*Børsen*, May 30, 2007). Running-in problems continued and apparently surpassed acceptable levels in 2007, which led the Group to take over operations at the Kladno packaging and processing plant in the Czech Republic on March 1, 2008 (700 employees; the buildings and equipment were already owned by the Group).

In addition to productivity and capacity utilization issues, Flextronics wanted to relocate production to optimize scale following its takeover of Solectron, which, according to EVP Iqbal "Bali" Padda, changed the partner's outlook. "Kladno no longer had strategic value to them (Flextronics) so they requested to relocate production" (*Børsen*, February 20, 2008). However, the Kladno site held strategic value for the LEGO Group, not only due to its proximity to the Group's large European market but also because the plant was located next to the Group's prototyping plant which created considerable synergies. Most importantly, Kladno was near the Group's new pan-European distribution center in Jirny, near Prague. Consequently, in July 2008 the company announced that the existing outsourcing agreement with Flextronics would be phased out during 2009 and that headquarters would again take over LEGO production in Juárez, Mexico and Nyíregyháza, Hungary. According to the press release, the LEGO Group concluded "that it is more optimal for the LEGO Group to manage the global manufacturing setup ourselves. With this decision, the LEGO supply chain will be developed faster through going for the best, leanest and highest quality solution at all times" (www.lego.com). The collaboration with Flextronics had allowed the Group to relocate production facilities to Kladno quickly and efficiently. However, the decision to insource certain production processes reflected the fact that the Group considered molding plastic bricks to be a strategic asset and that the company believed the out-sourcing of these activities did not constitute the most appropriate setup.

In sum, the severity and depth of the LEGO Group's crisis had required a major restructuring program, which entailed massive layoffs at its facilities in Denmark. Yet, in the end, the financial restoration was completed with relatively few layoffs. In 2005, no employee in the Group was in doubt that the company's existence was at stake. Management had, in this turnaround situation, relayed crystal-clear messages and established a sense of urgency through direct and honest communication. CEO Jørgen Vig Knudstorp had been instrumental in terms of his personal involvement in these communication efforts.

As it was now in financially good shape, the LEGO Group faced the challenge of identifying the best communicative forms and instruments that would allow it to maintain momentum and develop the internal organization. According to management, it was challenging to create and shape a common understanding of the desired future position through communication when innovation and growth were on the strategic agenda. Complacency was, perhaps, the Group's worst enemy.[7]

PRODUCT DEVELOPMENT: ENGAGING USERS AND RETAILERS

A situation in which various customers spontaneously establish brand communities to discuss, endorse, and embark on their own proprietary product development without getting paid for their efforts must be a dream scenario for most companies. However, for the LEGO Group it took some time to appreciate the fact that drawing on the experiences and ideas of thousands of LEGO fans could actually enrich product development and decision making, and provide the company with valuable feedback. The Group had a long history of pursuing lawsuits

[7] Interview with Christian Iversen, Executive Vice-President, Corporate Centre, March 12, 2008.

against companies and people who unlawfully used the LEGO brand or its products. However, by 2008 the close interaction with customers had come to be regarded as a key strategic asset that provided the Group with "valuable insight into consumer wishes and behavior" (LEGO Annual Report, 2007).

Today, inviting users to directly co-design new products or encouraging their involvement in online brand communities, where users discuss or seek inspiration, are integrated parts of the LEGO Group's business model.[8] However, the business model forced the Group to rethink ways of monitoring these communities and handling the interfaces between internal and external product development efforts.

First, LEGO employees – particularly product developers – had to acknowledge that the product development process and product launches could not solely be based on inside-out thinking, i.e., in-house development, market analysis, and research. Adoption of an outside-in perspective required that LEGO employees accept the fact that core users can make valuable contributions that could enhance the product development processes. In addition, proactively engaging user communities increased the level of exposure in various discussion groups and in other fora such as blogs, but these debates were hard to monitor or control. The company's main concern was whether these discussions and exchanges of ideas genuinely supported the brand and values of creativity, quality, and fun.

In fact, close interaction with its customers required the LEGO Group to maintain a rigid distinction between in-house management and user community support. Conventional management, monitoring, and control systems were simply not the right tools to help commun-ities flourish and inspire. On the contrary, to build stronger bonds, the Group needed to find ways to build trust, restate its values, and improve user understanding. However, in many instances, according

---

[8] Lugnet is a community for LEGO fans (www.lugnet.com). The site has numerous sub-communities, in which fan groups interconnect via the internet to celebrate the brand, blog and organize competitions and events.

to a Senior Director of Business Development, the best thing was to refrain from doing anything at all.[9]

User involvement occurred on many levels, in many programs, and with varying degrees of engagement and rules. Originally prevalent in adult user communities, *LEGO Factory* encouraged children to build and publish their own designs by using LEGO Digital Designer Software. Another, more organized, example was the LEGO Group's Ambassador Program, "a community based program made up of adult LEGO hobbyists who share their product and build expertise with the world-wide LEGO community and the public" (www.lego.com). Each year, the Group selected a few people whom it believed would best exemplify the program's fundamentals of building proficiency, enthusiasm, and professionalism toward the public (i.e., fans and employees of the LEGO Group). LEGO Certified Professionals was yet another exclusive community. It consisted of six people who were officially recognized by the LEGO Group as trusted business partners. They were LEGO hobbyists who had turned their passion for building and creating with LEGO bricks into a full-time or part-time profession (www.lego.com).

The LEGO Group's largest global retail clients – Wal-Mart and Toys "R" Us – were invited twice a year during what the LEGO Group termed "product input windows" to comment on the product portfolio prior to launch. The retailers could provide input on certain factors, such as the specific composition of robots and helicopters across the assortment, and provide their views on different price points. In return, the Group informed retailers about the extent to which their ideas and input had been incorporated into the final product portfolio.

LEGO Mindstorms 2.0 and NXT

Shortly after LEGO Mindstorms was launched in 1998, it became a huge success with more than one million sets sold. This prompted

---

[9] M. Hatch and M. Schultz, *Taking Brand Initiative: How Companies Align Strategy, Culture and Identity Through Corporate Branding.* San Francisco: Jossey-Bass, 2008.

plans for a second generation of robotic construction toys. Named "NXT" and launched in 2006, the second generation was partly designed by the lead users of Mindstorms.[10] While the first version was targeted at adults, LEGO wanted to extend the target group to include children. This required a simplified programming language, as well as a reduction in the number of bricks and the time needed to build one robot.

What was perhaps more interesting was the way the LEGO Group engaged an exclusive group of lead users to form a Mindstorms User Panel (MUP). The MUP was deeply involved in the "engine room" to innovate, design, and write program codes for next-generation Mindstorms. After the development of a prototype, numerous beta testers scrutinized the product intensively to provide the LEGO Group with feedback before a more commercial launch. In parallel with the official programming language, a user-developed software program had been developed within the Mindstorms community. The highly popular software allowed users to type their own programming codes, which in turn enabled them to make more assorted and more flexible robots. At first, the LEGO Group was skeptical, but it later realized the benefits of this development. Experiments completed by core users often made the product more stimulating and exciting. The Mindstorms community was vibrant and dynamic, with users writing books and manuals on robot building for dissemination among other core users.

User involvement in LEGO Mindstorms represented one important challenge that the LEGO Group needed to tackle and address – the fact that adult users were well-skilled in designing products for adults. They were able to construct complex show models but paid less attention to products that were saleable. Mindstorms NXT was successful. According to EVP Mads Nipper, however, the involvement of children in the product development process still constituted a key challenge for the LEGO Group.

[10] The engagement of lead users is more thoroughly described in Brendan I. Koerner, "Geeks in toyland," *Wired Magazine,* February 2006, www.wired.com/wired/archive/14.02/lego.html.

DIGITALIZATION: CAPTURING NEW BUSINESS OPPORTUNITIES

Digitalization and virtual reality were by no means unknown concepts in the LEGO Group's business vocabulary. Since the mid-1990s, the company had, with varying degrees of success, explored business opportunities enabled by technological advancements. In the mid-1990s, the Group was under pressure from various computer game producers to create games for use on the Nintendo GameCube and Sony PlayStation consoles. This led to attempts to digitalize the bricks. In 1997, the LEGO Group established the subsidiary LEGO Media International in London, the purpose of which was to develop and sell LEGO computer games, video films, and books. Various computer games were introduced to target different age groups – LEGO Friends for girls, LEGO Racer for boys, and LEGO Rock Racers for adults. Millions were invested in in-house software development in Milan, London, and San Francisco. Although initial sales were promising, they could not compensate for the high development costs. Consequently, the Group downsized or closed its development departments and initiated a process to find companies to take over software development and sell LEGO computer games – companies that had years of experience and knowledge in the field.

The LEGO Group's initial efforts to stage the LEGO idea in the virtual world suffered further from an over-arching belief that a LEGO user in a virtual world would be fundamentally different from original LEGO users. In reality, these users were similar and shared the same fundamental passion for the LEGO idea and brand. In fact, the LEGO Group learned that the most hardcore LEGO users of the physical bricks were also front-runners in testing and adapting to new technologies. In the late 1990s, new digital product concepts were introduced. The strong emphasis on technology blurred how the virtual experience could bridge and enhance the more physical LEGO experience. From a commercial perspective, it was difficult to profit from digital product ideas.[11]

---

[11] Interview with Lisbeth Valther Pallesen, March 11, 2008.

Ten years later, the LEGO Group found itself confronting the same challenges. First, the company needed to explore how to create and balance virtual content, experiences, and ideas that would boost sales of physical LEGO products. This was much like the relationship between books and films in terms of how one experience can bolster and stimulate the other. To get this equation right, the Group examined its successes – LEGO Star Wars and Indiana Jones – and analyzed how these computer games had bolstered sales of the physical product lines. The latter was expected to surpass sales of DKK 500 million in 2008 (*Børsen*, June 6, 2008). The Group's success with digitalization would depend on the extent to which the company could achieve *seamless integration* between the virtual and physical worlds. Second, the Group had to confront the simple challenge of turning the "digital formula" into a profitable business. Given the success of social communities and networks on the Internet, the LEGO Group aspired to unite an indefinite number of LEGO users in a proper universe. However, for this business model to be sustainable, users would have to pay for the experience.

Integration of play: LEGO Universe

Along with the development of core product lines, the company began working on what was possibly its largest digital venture in years in 2006, namely *LEGO Universe* – a massive multiplayer online game (MMOG) in which thousands of LEGO fans would create, build, quest, and socialize in a game world that would constantly evolve through players' actions (www.lego.com). The company's other growth levers – geographical expansion in India, China, and the USA, and additional sales and development of core products – entailed low/medium risk and medium profit potential. In comparison, new digital product invention was a high-risk activity that had the potential for extraordinarily high returns if the right product was found.

Inspired by blockbuster MMOG successes like *World of Warcraft* and *Ragnarok*, the LEGO Group aimed to create a game space where millions of LEGO aficionados could create and communicate via integrated chat functions. Connected via multiple servers scattered around the world, thousands of users could participate and play simultaneously. Normally, an MMOG does not have an ultimate aim but is based on an epic or theatrical narrative with numerous challenges, levels, and collaborations. According to Executive Vice-President Lisbeth Valther Pallesen, the social aspect was pivotal: "The internet connects people and creates a kind of contact and dialogue. The children of today are social via the internet; they are actually connected to many peers, and the technology enables them to keep track of all of the contacts" (*Børsen*, April 16, 2008).

The LEGO Group outsourced its game development activities in the late 1990s and subsequently gained success with Star Wars. With LEGO Universe, however, the company was extensively involved in design, development, and operation, which it undertook together with its game development partner NetDevil. According to the Group, NetDevil supported its brand values and the Group's special contact with LEGO enthusiasts. In addition, fifty core adult fans were directly involved in the development of LEGO Universe, while a representative segment of the Group's target groups, mainly children, were continually involved in user tests. The Group expected to launch the Universe in 2009 and base the business model on subscriptions. Advertisements were not slated to serve as a source of income. By the end of 2008, 2.5 million users had already registered.

The LEGO Group's transformation over the past five years had been eventful and highly emotional. The company was in good shape after completing a successful turnaround and the platform for future growth had been subsequently crafted and designed. Recent financial results proved the strength of this strategic master plan (Table 3.1). During the transformation, the Group went from a vertically integrated business model to experimenting with new organizational forms in various parts of the value chain. Touching upon the Group's future, Knudstorp noted: "We have gone through a period marked by inside focus and perspective. Now it is time to open up and establish new relations. I would like to see us enter into new partnerships with exciting companies and people. We need to seek new ways proactively, but exactly how I do not know today. Things are not black and white, and that is essentially the challenge" (*Berlingske Tidende*, August 31, 2008).

Whether the LEGO Group's organizational experiments dealt with offshoring or outsourcing, customer involvement or digital ventures, they fundamentally challenged and redefined the boundaries of the company. On the one hand, the Group was exposed to useful ideas and inspiration from various stakeholder environments, while on the other hand, the more disintegrated business model (network model) implied a more rigid focus on transaction costs and how to capitalize on new stakeholder relations.

LEGO: SUMMARY AND QUESTIONS FOR DISCUSSION

The LEGO Group is a story of a dramatic turnaround in a privately owned company having a highly recognized and well-reputed global brand. It is a company that lost faith in its core ideas when it was confronted with a changing marketplace and the emergence of new technologies. The rise of digital games and toys, such as the Game Boy and the PlayStation, during the 1990s made the company question whether the kids of the future had the patience to engage in LEGO play, and if parents had the willingness to pay for the multicolored bricks that, compared with many other kinds of plastic toys, were still very expensive. This loss of self-confidence made the company extend the brand into areas and technologies where it had little in-house expertise and unclear ideas of what it meant to take the LEGO idea into areas of play other than construction play. In addition, the company invested heavily in licensed products, such as Harry Potter, which created a much more volatile turnover, as they depended much more on the release of new movies and merchandise, etc.

The depth of the crisis that followed urged the company to look for new solutions and engage in a critical scrutiny of many of its taken-for-granted assumptions, which was the springboard for the innovation of its managerial and organizational practices. The crisis forced the new management team headed by Jørgen Vig Knudstorp to innovate, but it was by looking into the past and the true LEGO values that they realized how to best move forward with the LEGO brand. Thus, management innovation may well depart from a reinterpretation of past achievements and reflections about what made the company successful and innovative in the first place. One of the fundamental changes in the midst of the crisis was that the company decided to open up its boundaries and create a new mindset with a closer collaboration and engagement of its business partners and consumers. Also, it engaged in an extensive outsourcing of its supply chain. Not all of these openings turned out to be as radical as first predicted, and eventually the outsourcing was less comprehensive than first anticipated. As such, the case facilitates discussion of the following questions:

1. What were the most significant management innovations undertaken by the new management team in the LEGO Group?
   a. What did they do differently in their business practices in their supply chain?
   b. What changed in their relationship with their end consumers?
   c. How did they start to collaborate in new ways with their big customers among the retailers? What changed in terms of the boundaries between the organization and the environment?
   d. What did they learn in the process of innovating? Which management innovations were taken further during the turnaround? Why did they not continue outsourcing?
   e. How did their management innovations influence the LEGO brand?
2. One example of radical change was the opening of the organization toward adult fans, inviting them to take part in the co-creation of new products and games and at times even the fundamental ideas of LEGO play. In addition, they developed a much closer relationship to their big customers. Very often new ideas were generated by outside stakeholders, but had to be executed by the people from the LEGO Group.

a. What are the risks involved in engaging external stakeholders in co-creation?

b. What are the cultural changes necessary to make co-creation work?

c. What are the implications of co-creation for the roles of top management and middle managers?

3. How did the opening of the boundaries of the LEGO Group influence the LEGO brand?

a. How did external stakeholders contribute to the revitalization of the classic LEGO ideas?

b. What were the implications for brand management?

4. Looking at the development of the digitalization of LEGO play and the growing importance of the social media, which areas of management innovation could be envisioned for the LEGO Group in the future?

a. In particular, what will be the likely effect of the LEGO Group's venture LEGO Universe on the organization of the LEGO Group in the future?

ADDITIONAL SOURCES IN RELATION TO THE LEGO GROUP

LEGO Ambassasdors (2010)
www.lego.com/eng/info/default.asp?page=ambassadors.
LEGO fans:
www.lugnet.com
www.firstlegoleague.org/

Antorini, Y. M. (2007) *Brand Community Innovation – An Intrinsic Study of the Adult Fan of LEGO Community*. Copenhagen: Samfundslitteratur.

Hatch, M. and Schultz, M. (2009) "Of bricks and brands. From corporate to enterprise branding," *Organizational Dynamics*, 38(2), 117–30.

Hatch, M. and Schultz, M. (2008) *Taking Brand Initiative: How Companies Align Strategy, Culture and Identity Through Corporate Branding*. San Francisco: Jossey-Bass.

Koerner, B. I. (2006) "Geeks in toyland," *Wired Magazine*, 14.02 – February.

Larsen, M. M., Pedersen T., and Slepniov, D. (2010). *LEGO Group: An Outsourcing Journey*. Ivey Publishing, Case: 9B10M094.

Oliver, K., Samakh, E., and Heckmann, P (2006) "Rebuilding Lego, brick by brick," *Strategy & Business*, August.

Robertson, D. and Crawford, R. (2008) "Innovation at the LEGO Group," IMD-380-382, Institute for Management Development, Lausanne, Switzerland.

Schultz, M. and Hatch, M. J. (2003) "The cycles of corporate branding: The case of LEGO Company," *California Management Review*, 45(1), 6–26.

4   Vestas: The will to win(d)

It was with a sense of ambiguity that Ditlev Engel, CEO of the Danish wind turbine manufacturer Vestas Wind Systems, gave his speech at the annual meeting of the Confederation of Danish Industries in 2007. On the one hand, he saw the annual meeting as a unique opportunity to propagate key messages about Vestas and its global role in defining modern energy. On the other hand, he found himself in front of an audience with backgrounds in various industrial companies, companies that had characteristics different from those of Vestas. He pondered whether they fully grasped the dynamics of the wind industry and the global challenges facing Vestas. Of course, Vestas enjoyed the attention and interest it received from business practitioners, the political community, and the general public. In fact, it was one of the most traded stocks on the Copenhagen Stock Exchange and had a relatively large number of private investors as shareholders. Within the Confederation of Danish Industries, it was regarded as one of the crown jewels with respect to technology and know-how. However, while it acknowledged its affiliation with those companies within the Confederation, Vestas's self-understanding, mindset and modus operandi were more similar to those of IT companies. These companies typically operated with growth scenarios of 30 percent per annum and swift decision-making processes. Touching upon this dilemma in his speech, Engel explained:

> In Denmark, 20 per cent of our energy is from wind power. That number surprises and impresses people all over the world. Is 20 per cent that much? Yes. On a global level, the figure is 0.7 per cent. So there's room for improvement or great possibilities. That's why energy is high on the world's agenda right now. Much has been happening. We heard from the EU that 20 per cent of our energy in

2020 must come from renewable energy. In the US, the new energy law is subject to much discussion. The House of Representatives suggests that in 2020, 15 per cent of electricity should come from renewable energy. If we then go to China, they've raised their percentage of renewable energy from 8 per cent to 15 per cent. According to *China Daily* and China itself, this corresponds to an investment of $265 billion. The focus is on wind and water. If we compare these numbers to the 0.7 per cent, then everyone can see what our world is like at Vestas, and why we sometimes feel that the agenda is off track compared to the big picture. (President and CEO Ditlev Engel, Annual Meeting of the Confederation of Danish Industries, September 2007)

Despite politicians' receptiveness and sympathetic attitudes, Vestas did not always feel that they fully understood the big picture. When the Australian government announced its refusal to raise the mandatory renewable energy target (MRET), which was initially designed to support industrial growth, wind power advocates argued that billions of dollars in potential investment would evaporate. Vestas, for example, would reconsider its plans to build a turbine blade manufacturing plant in Tasmania, a multimillion dollar investment. Another example involved its application to install a number of test turbines off the Danish shore. The offshore market was a strategic priority but the turbines needed further testing prior to large-scale market penetration. When referring the issue to a committee, politicians had discussed it animatedly. However, as of spring 2008 no defining decision had been made, which stretched Vestas's patience.

Furthermore, Vestas's self-image of a "fast-running gazelle" needed to settle internally. With its massive growth in revenue, employee intake, new production sites, and R&D facilities, Vestas's business platform had become more complex in recent years. The key was to inculcate the self-image of a modern, next-generation wind power maker in the minds of employees, providers, and societies without sounding hollow. Undoubtedly, Vestas's management team was perfectly aware of the company's identity aspirations and it used every occasion to communicate and convey the self-image of proliferation. The challenge, however, was to reach the outermost parts of the company. How could management get all employees to buy into the self-image of proliferation and its implications on conduct? How could employees and middle management be infused with the right dose of confidence to confront future challenges? The majority of Vestas's middle management team was comprised of engineers who were highly skilled professionals, but they did not always feel confident when communicating critical messages to an audience.

Important steps were taken when Engel took over at the helm in 2005, steps which included the formulation of a new strategy named "The Will to Win," the crafting of a new vision and mission, a reshuffle of the organization followed by substantial investments in personnel development, and stakeholder management – all initiatives that helped to reshape Vestas into the biggest wind turbine maker in the world. However, according to the CEO, the company was not even halfway through its reshaping: "We are standing on a burning platform. Expectations will continue to intensify and we have to live up to those expectations. It is challenging now and it will be challenging in the future. We are not near to where we will be. There is a long way to go" (*RB-Børsen*, February 27, 2008, published in *ErhvervsBladet*).

A BRIEF HISTORY OF VESTAS

Vestas was founded in 1945 as VEstjysk STaal Teknik A/S, which was quickly abbreviated to "Vestas." The company primarily produced household appliances and agricultural equipment, including ploughshares and rubber tractors, but throughout the 1950s, 1960s, and 1970s, the company extended its product range to include vacuum tankers, crop sprayers, intercoolers, and lightweight cranes. Most of its products were exported.

Booming energy prices and supply shortages in the 1970s led Vestas to look into the potential for wind turbines as an alternative, clean source of energy. Following numerous experiments, the company delivered its first windmill in 1979 and initiated serial production of wind turbines in 1980, which was further favored by auspicious political winds and anti-nuclear movements. In 1986, it learned the hard way that the industry was (and still is) highly dependent on the political climate. Special tax laws, which had made it advantageous to build wind turbines in California, lapsed in late 1985 and early 1986, which in turn forced Vestas to suspend its payments. Common logic would suggest that it was unwise to rescue the company. In 1986, a barrel of oil sold at US$14, while the turbines could only produce 30 kWh per hour and turbine production needed to be located close to the markets, i.e., in high-cost areas like Denmark and Germany. Nevertheless, seventy Danish patriots, all sharing the same passion in wind as an energy source, revitalized the company and named it Vestas Wind Systems A/S. In November 1991, Vestas erected its 1,000th turbine in Denmark. Following years of solid development, Vestas went public on the Copenhagen Stock Exchange in 1998. A merger with another Danish-based turbine maker, NEG Micon, in 2004 made Vestas the world leader in the wind energy market. At that point, it had the largest market share and a turnover of €2.5 billion (see Table 4.1 and Figure 4.1). Following the merger, Vestas experienced some financial troubles, which prompted changes in management. On May 1, 2005, Ditlev Engel became CEO.

Industry, markets, and competitors

Shifting political atmospheres and increasing climate concerns have had a notable impact on the development of wind energy. When a production tax credit (PTC) on windmills was interrupted in the USA, the amount of installed megawatts dropped 67 percent in 2004. It then skyrocketed by 400 percent when the PTC was renewed in 2005. The entire industry was favored by strong environmental concerns, sky-high oil prices, and gas prices that improved the competitiveness of wind energy. In the USA, Europe, India, and China, governments promoted strong supportive policies on the back of climate change concerns (see Box 4.1 for the planned regional implementation and a discussion of political incentives).

Table 4.1 *Financial highlights and key ratios*

	2007	2006	2005	2004	2003*	2002*
Income statement (€ million)						
Revenue	4,861	3,854	3,583	2,363	1,653	1,395
Gross profit	825	461	84	120	150	142
Operating profit before financial income and expenses, depreciation and amortization (EBITDA)	579	328	9	64	142	124
Operating profit/(loss) (EBIT)	443	201	(116)	(49)	74	74
Profit/(loss) of financial items	0	161	(158)	(89)	53	60
Profit/(loss) before tax	443	161	(158)	(89)	54	60
Profit/(loss) for the year	291	111	(192)	(61)	36	45
Revenue growth (%)						
Annual growth in revenue	26.1	7.6	51.6	43	18.5	–
Cash flows and investments (€ million)						
Cash flow from operating activities	701	598	148	(30)	153	(126)
Cash flow from investing activities	(317)	(144)	(137)	(201)	(119)	3
Cash flow from financing activities	(54)	(54)	(101)	(137)	(201)	(119)
Change in cash and cash equivalents less current portion of bank debt	330	353	(35)	227	15	(106)
Key ratios (%)						
Gross margin	17	12	2.4	5.1	9.1	10.2
EBITDA	11.9	8.5	0.3	5	8.6	8.9

Table 4.1 (*cont.*)

	2007	2006	2005	2004	2003*	2002*
Operating profit margin (EBIT)	9.1	5.2	(3.2)	(2.1)	4.5	5.3
Return on invested capital (ROIC)	30.9	11.9	(13.2)	(3.8)	8.1	9.6
Solvency ratio	35.3	34.5	31.2	40.3	44.1	47
Return on equity	21	10	(18.1)	(6.9)	5.9	7.8
Gearing	9.9	13.8	51.2	50.1	40.4	44.5
Share data (%)						
Earnings per share	1.6	0.6	(1.1)	(0.5)	0.3	0.4
P/E-value	47.1	52.8	(12.7)	(18.2)	38.6	21.9
Dividend per share	0	0	0	0	0	0.1
Share price December 31 (euros)	74	32	13.9	8.8	13.1	9.4
Employees						
Average number of employees	13.820	11.334	10.300	9.449	6.394	5.974
Revenue per full-time employee (FTE) (€ million)	0.35	0.34	0.35	0.25	0.26	0.23

Source: Vestas annual reports

* Financial highlights for 2002–3 have not been restated to reflect the new accounting policies, nor do they contain the figures for NEG Micon A/S and therefore correspond to the financial highlights presented in the Annual Report for 2004. The adjustments that would be necessary if the comparative figures in the financial highlights for 2002–3 were to be restated to IFRS correspond to the adjustments made in the opening balance sheet as of January 1, 2004.

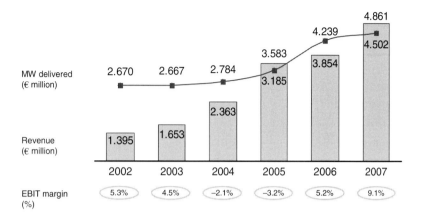

Source: Vestas Annual Report, 2007

FIGURE 4.1 MW delivered, revenue, and EBIT margins, 2002–7

BOX 4.1   **Region-based political incentives**

Europe

The EU is showing strong commitment to supporting renewable energy generation through its adhesion to the Kyoto Protocol. In a nutshell, the Protocol aims to: (1) Cut greenhouse gas emissions by 20 percent in 2020 relative to 1990, and (2) generate 20 percent of total energy from renewable sources by 2020 (against 6.5 percent in 2006). Europe is thus the largest market for wind power to 2011, capturing 45 percent of wind power MW capacity additions. There are several ways to achieve these ambitious targets, but most European governments (i.e., Austria, Belgium, Denmark, France, Germany, the Netherlands, Portugal, and Spain) have put in place feed-in tariff policies, in which utilities are obliged to enable renewable energy plants to connect to the electricity grid and must purchase any electricity generated by renewable resources at fixed minimum prices.

BOX 4.1 (CONTINUED)

The USA

The federal government promotes renewable energy through a PTC, which provides a ten-year credit of US$19/MWh (inflation adjusted) for green power. Increasingly, states such as California and Texas are implementing incentive programs in addition to the federal policy, an indication that global warming is becoming a major concern in the USA. California is considering bringing forward the goal to generate 20 percent of its renewable energy in total energy from 2010 to 2020 (compared with 10 percent in 2004) and setting a higher target for 2020 of 33 percent renewable energy. The PTC has had a decisive impact on new MW installed, given the low competitiveness of wind energy relative to fossil energy. Each time the fiscal incentive program was not renewed (2001, 2002, and 2004), the addition of new capacities in wind energy fell dramatically. The current PTC policy ran until the end of 2008 and its extension to 2013 was passed in August 2007 in the House of Representatives and now awaits approval from the Senate. Should the PTC policy not be renewed, the impact would be negative in the short term but negligible in the medium term, as (1) the USA needs ever more power generation capacities, (2) polluting electricity sources are under increasing pressure, and (3) even China is putting in place a proactive renewable energy policy.

Asia (mainly China and India)

Environmentally friendly policies are progressively being implemented, with the Chinese government planning to install 30,000 MW of wind energy by 2020 and the Indian government installing 10,000 MW by 2010. Each incentive policy is a mix of tax measures and renewable portfolio standards (RPS) that oblige utilities to generate a certain amount of their output from renewable energy: The Chinese new Renewable Energy Law required the local utilities to secure 5 percent of their total electricity output from renewable energy by 2010 and 10 percent by 2020, which represents a major

BOX 4.1 (CONTINUED)

investment effort, considering the growth prospects seen for Chinese fossil-fuelled power generation assets. We expect the strong momentum in political incentives to continue. Governments are putting pressure on fossil-fuel pollutants in order to meet ambitious renewable energy targets. In Europe, after member countries granted free CO_2 emissions quotas too generously for 2005–7, the Commission has imposed more stringent quota allocations for 2008–12. An increasingly vocal group (which includes Germany's environment minister, Sigmar Gabriel) is proposing an end to free emission quotas after 2012, suggesting that they are put up for auction instead. For 2008–12, Germany has already decided to put 10 percent of its quotas up for auction. Consequently, a ton of CO_2, currently worth nothing, is likely to become ever more expensive.

Source: Vestas Annual Report, 2007

Despite aggressive growth in both the USA and Asia (China and India), Europe remained the leading market for wind energy, representing 61 percent (or 57,000 MW) of accumulated installed capacity at the end of 2007. Forecasts for the number of wind power installations worldwide by 2020 were impressive. Industry analysts did not feel that 1,000,000 MW of cumulative installed base wind turbines by 2020 was unrealistic. This needed to be compared to the 94,000 MW of installed capacity by the end of 2007 (HSBC Global Research, Equity Report, September 14, 2007). In 2007, European wind capacity grew by 8,500 MW – a growth of more than 17 percent from the previous year. In terms of new installations, the USA maintained its leadership position with 5,244 MW of new installations, followed by Spain and China, which added 3,515 MW and 3,400 MW to their total capacities, respectively. In terms of capacity installed, China was the fastest growing market for wind energy in the world (see Table 4.2).

An exceedingly favorable political environment, coupled with promising growth rates for wind energy in general, sparked a

Table 4.2 *Market growth in selected markets*

	MW Ultimo				Growth	
	2004	2005	2006	2007	2006–7 (percentage)	Three-year average
Germany	16.649	18.445	20.652	22.277	7.9	10.2
USA	6.750	9.181	11.635	16.879	45.1	35.7
Spain	8.263	10.027	11.614	14.714	26.7	21.2
India	3.000	4.388	6.228	7.845	26	37.8
China	769	1.264	2.588	5.875	127	97
Denmark	3.083	3.087	3.101	3.088	−0.4	0.1
Italy	1.264	1.713	2.118	2.721	28.5	29.2
France	386	775	1.585	2.471	56	85.7
UK	889	1.336	1.967	2.394	21.7	39.1
Portugal	585	1.087	1.716	2.150	25.3	54.3
Ten biggest accumulated	41.634	51.303	63.203	80.415	27.2	24.5

Source: BTM Consult (published in *Børsen*, March 31, 2008)

substantial interest in entering the industry. Vestas's competitors were a mixture of family-owned businesses (Enercon GmbH), listed companies (Gamesa, Suzlon, Nordex, and Repower), and divisions of large conglomerates (GE Wind and Siemens). In addition, the growing wind power market in China encouraged domestic production of wind turbines. Approximately forty Chinese companies were involved in the manufacturing of wind turbines, which were springing up like mushrooms across the country, with Goldwind showing itself to be the dominant player (see Box 4.2). While incumbents gradually sought to build larger, more technologically advanced wind turbines, the entrance of Chinese turbine makers revived the construction of smaller, less technologically intense wind turbines that were easier to transport in areas with poor infrastructures.

BOX 4.2 **Competitive landscape**

Gamesa

Gamesa, the Spanish-based wind turbine manufacturer, was originally founded as Gamesa Eólica – a joint venture in 1994 by Vestas and the Gamesa Corporation. The company quickly gained success selling windmills to the Spanish energy sector. In 2001 Vestas decided to sell its 40 percent stock to the Gamesa Corporation. Gamesa is now a focused wind generator manufacturer as the company divested its solar business unit in the beginning of 2008. The company is the market leader in Spain and the world's second largest producer with a 15.6 percent market share in 2006. Gamesa's product range includes primarily two turbine types: 850 KW and 2.0 MW. Contrary to most turbine manufacturers, Gamesa is strongly vertically integrated, which gives it greater independence from external suppliers and makes it less vulnerable to bottlenecks in key components, primarily gear boxes and large bearings. Iberdrola, the world's biggest wind farm operator, owns 25 percent of Gamesa's capital.

GE Wind

GE Wind, GE Energy's wind division, was the world's third-largest manufacturer of wind turbines with a market share of approximately 15.5 percent in 2006. GE Wind leads the US market and has devoted many resources to developing and selling large mills ranging from 1.5 to 3.6 MW turbines. GE Wind is poorly vertically integrated; however, being part of the GE conglomerate enables the company to secure its supply chain, i.e., financial resources and negotiating power with suppliers.

Enercon GmbH

The German-based wind turbine manufacturer Enercon GmbH holds a dominant position in its home market (50.2 percent market share in 2007). The company produces primarily large mills (operating, for example, a 6 MW turbine) and focuses on innovation. It invented the gearless wind turbine, which supposedly is more reliable than traditional

BOX 4.2 (CONTINUED)

turbines with gear boxes. Despite innovation efforts toward large mills, it still produces small turbines down to 330 KW. With respect to branding, the company is known for painting the base of the towers light green to mix in with the terrain and has turbine housings in a drop shaped form designed by world-renowned architect and designer Norman Foster.

Siemens Wind (Bonus Energy)

Siemens entered the wind energy business in December 2004 acquiring Bonus Energy. Like GE, the company has been able to use the conglomerate brand to increase sales and global dispersion of Bonus Energy. In 2007, the company experienced a 56 percent growth in sales. Siemens Wind has for many years focused on offshore mills – a segment of the market that Vestas has wished to enter but has not yet succeeded due to technical difficulties in late 2007. Furthermore, Siemens owns the gear box producer Winergy (with a 40 percent market share of the gear box market), leaving the wind division less vulnerable to sudden changes in production capacities.

Suzlon Energy

The Indian-based company Suzlon Energy was founded in 1995 and is the largest emergent market windmill producer with a global market share of approximately 8 percent. Even though India is their home market, international marketing is headed from Århus, Denmark, while the management HQ is located in Amsterdam. Suzlon Energy bought Hansen Transmission in 2006, giving it a 30 percent share of the gear box market. Thus, two-thirds of the global gear box market is controlled by Vestas's competitors. Suzlon is market leader in India and produces turbines from 350 KW to 2 MW.

Goldwind

Goldwind, the Chinese manufacturer of windmills, was founded in 1997 and is market leader in China, with Vestas coming in second.

BOX 4.2 (CONTINUED)

Having knowledge of the varying geography and climate in China, the company has focused on developing specific turbine types for different temperatures and its best-selling turbine (600 KW) exists in three different temperature versions. In 2007 the company's product portfolio consisted of turbines ranging from 600 KW to 1.5 MW.

Source: Vestas Annual Report, 2007

STAGE SHIFT NO. 1: THE WILL TO WIN

"An unpolished diamond" with enormous potential – this was Engel's initial perception of the company he was asked to lead in October 2004. He took the helm in February 2005. His first two months as CEO were rather unconventional. While the Chairman of the Board Bent Erik Carlsen and former CEO Svend Sigaard still fronted the company, Engel visited various production and sales sites around the world to probe local plant managers and factory workers about their daily challenges. Based on their honest opinions and input, he was able to gather, digest, and examine his own impressions, which were subsequently documented in his personal notes. These laid the foundation for his plan for Vestas entitled "The Will to Win." Presented in May 2005, the strategic action plan contained elements designed to strengthen Vestas's financial results and long-term development by: (1) Improving the profit margin to at least 10 percent; (2) reducing net working capital to a maximum of 20–25 percent; and (3) obtaining a global market share of at least 35 percent. The plan also broke with the traditional perception of wind power as an alternative source of energy. Engel explained: "Many people regard wind power and thereby Vestas as a 'romantic flirt' with alternative energy sources. It is not. Vestas and wind power is a real and very competitive alternative to oil and gas ... I put my foot down each time I see wind in various energy reports mentioned in the section for renewable energy. I want wind to have its own section on [a] par with oil and gas" (*Berlingske News Magazine*, June 3, 2005 and "The Will to Win"). The idea of building up and nurturing an image as a "deadly serious energy supplier" was encapsulated in the company's simple vision: *Wind, Oil, and Gas*. Vestas wanted to challenge the common perception that wind power was chosen "on account of environmental considerations" and "in spite of economic concerns," and instead strove to have wind energy perceived on a par with oil and gas. The vision also expressed the ambitious target for employees to take the company to a new level. The fact that wind power was mentioned first in the vision confirmed the challenge at hand.

In addition, the company's mission – *failure is not an option* – challenged potential complacency within the organization. "Good enough" was regarded as a relative term. Every employee was asked to genuinely do his or her best in every task performed. If employees discovered irregularities or inappropriate conduct that could damage Vestas's finances or reputation, they were encouraged to report them for further investigation. This procedure was systematized in a whistleblower function following the implementation of the new strategic plan.

The mission implicitly formulated Vestas's ambitious promise to provide reliable, operational wind turbines, and high service levels. As put more provocatively by the CEO: "Who wants a television that flickers? It is extremely annoying" (*Berlingske News Magazine*, March 30, 2007). A common misunderstanding of the mission statement was that Vestas did not accept errors. However, given its operations in a highly technological, innovative industry, risks were not uncommon. Therefore, the mission called for preparation and deliberated risk management to better curb the risk of failure. Acting as the glue that held everything together and as guidelines for everyday work, Vestas used its four core values: Trustworthiness, care, the power to act, and development. These values embodied the company's aspirations of keeping its promises to customers, prioritizing safety and quality, and demonstrating a willingness to *act* differently without necessarily *being* different. As a symbol of the company's culture and as a source of inspiration, former CEO Johannes Poulsen (1987–2002) had a sculpture designed and placed in front of headquarters entitled *Viljen* ("Willpower"). The sculpture appeared to reach for the sky, while the lower part was firmly anchored to the ground, expressing Vestas's vision and values in a compelling manner (see Box 4.3).

However, Vestas's transformation was not only about words and artifacts. "The Will to Win" strategy plan spawned a number of managerial and organizational initiatives, including Vestas's governance structure, the Vestas Government and the Vestas Constitution.

Governmental rhetoric

In order to obtain an update on the status of business operations, Vestas's management or *presidents* participated in weekly meetings, during which strategic and operational challenges related to each field of responsibility were discussed, as was the management of the thirteen *Constitution* projects. These *state-of-affairs* sessions also allowed for the sharing of key business information between the *Ministries* and helped to secure symmetric information among the presidents in the Vestas *Government*. The latter were then able to share updated information with middle management.

According to the CEO, the underlying reason for transforming Vestas's management structure into a political system with affiliated concepts and titles was rather simple: "As soon as you discuss the concept of management, people have an indefinite number of opinions and interpretations. Everybody has a much more unambiguous understanding of a political system. People understand the terminology of ministries, well-defined responsibility areas and the meaning of a constitution. This is absolutely key to align interests and to establish a common frame of reference in a global company like Vestas" (interview with Ditlev Engel, February 19, 2008). In Vestas's setup, there was no element of matrix figures or shared responsibility. To avoid fickle perceptions of roles and responsibilities and to maintain simplicity,

BOX 4.3   Vestas's vision, mission, and values

Vision: Wind, oil, and gas

With these words, Vestas signals the Group's intention, as a market leader, to assume a leadership role in the process of making wind a source of energy that is on a par with conventional energy sources such as oil and gas. This vision has been accepted by Vestas's customers and many political decision makers who create the framework for the industry.

A number of industry and social factors support developments toward achieving Vestas's vision, as wind power offers a number of clear benefits over other energy sources. The five most important benefits are as follows:

- Wind is an inexhaustible, free source of energy.
- Wind power can compete with conventional sources of energy in terms of cost.
- Wind power reduces dependence on imported energy.
- Wind power facilitates fast ramp-up of extensive production capacity.
- Wind power contributes to reducing CO_2 and other greenhouse gas emissions.

Today, these five arguments weigh heavily in all countries with an interest in wind power.

Mission: Failure is not an option

This is the simple wording of Vestas's mission, representing the basic course which is to help the Group achieve the goals defined in the strategy plan and to achieve the stated vision. In other words, Vestas does not apply the concept of "good enough." It must always be a reliable collaboration partner, supplier, and employer – at technical, financial, environmental, and personal levels. Its most important resource is the skills and the enthusiasm held by the Group's employees, and the mission underlines that everyone contributes the very best he or she can to achieve optimum results – and to win. At Vestas, no error is too small to act on.

BOX 4.3 (CONTINUED)

Values: Trustworthiness, care, the power to act, and development

Vestas's four core values provide the foundation for all the Group's activities and express its fundamental views on running a business. Vestas's own sculpture entitled "Willpower," which has been placed at a number of the Group's locations, symbolizes the company's values as it reaches for the sky but remains firmly anchored to the ground. Trustworthiness and care involve Vestas always keeping its promises, acting as a serious and careful partner relative to all stakeholders, and giving top priority to safety, quality, and respect in every context. Through the power to act and development, Vestas aims to ensure that it reaches its goals through constantly striving for new and better solutions for the benefit of the customers. Know-how and skills must be expanded through the ongoing development of employees and Group-wide collaboration in an organization that possesses the will to change and allows room for independent initiative, enabling each individual employee to always make the decision that serves Vestas best.

Source: www.vestas.com

Engel gathered the thirteen presidents for two days in 2005 to determine fields of responsibility. To these meetings he brought thirteen blank pieces of paperboard. Each president had to have one specific area of responsibility before the meeting was over (see Figure 4.2). Such a transparent process not only ensured that management was exceedingly engaged and committed but also created a strong internal understanding of who was responsible for which areas. The same kind of simplicity and transparency permeated business performance reviews and the crafting and presentation of business unit strategies. Engel wanted short (a maximum of four pages) and concise *memoranda* that described goals and means. He believed that this form of reporting strengthened the quality of discussion within the Vestas Government and that it also aligned expectations and set a common direction.

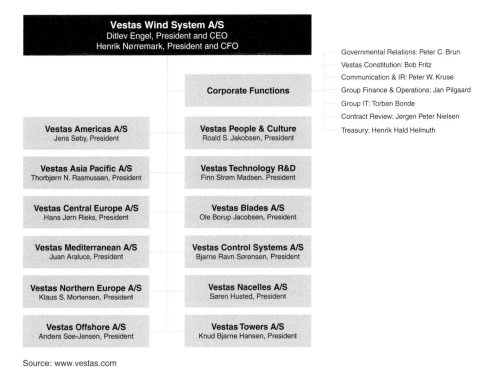

Source: www.vestas.com

FIGURE 4.2   Vestas Government and organizational structure

Robert P. Fritz and the Constitution

The Vestas Constitution, through which "The Will to Win" plan was installed and executed, played a critical role in turning the company around. The Constitution was comprised of thirteen enabling projects. While one group of projects had to do with creating "one Vestas" by highlighting knowledge sharing, information flows, and communication, other project streams involved practicing a global form of management and enhancing skill development, as exemplified by the introduction of the Six Sigma improvement tool to better cope with variability in process and performance measurements. A third group of initiatives aimed to improve overall performance in product and component quality, capacity understanding, and Vestas's approach to risk management. With the objective of increasing Vestas's capability, the fourth group of projects was targeted at producing wind turbines that lived up to customer expectations, which should in turn improve customer satisfaction. To that end, more systematic and better feedback from already installed turbines helped to fine-tune future installments.

All of these projects served as the foundation for translating the company's visionary thoughts and ideas into practice. However, the Vestas Constitution was more pervasive than simply staging and implementing change management and improvement projects. To Engel, the Constitution was fundamental and sustainable – a key document that described how Vestas's procedures and systems, as handled every day by employees, originated from some essential attitude or way of thinking (*Berlingske News Magazine*, March 30, 2007).

To spearhead the constitution-enabling projects, Vestas needed a forceful and highly effective resource that could facilitate implementation and ensure that engineers would buy into the company's transformation project. Engel was well aware that he lacked engineering skills and knowledge about the wind industry, so he hired Robert P. Fritz, a former Vice-President of FLP Energy in Florida, which was one of Vestas's key customers in the US market. Fritz added a good dose of technical credence to the projects and a strong customer orientation. As a customer, he had been one of Vestas's most severe critics, highlighting the long delivery times, technical flaws, and inadequate service levels. At the same time, he was probably one of the most knowledgeable persons within the industry and had a large number of installed turbines on his résumé. When he joined Vestas, he was given free rein to enter meetings abruptly, to challenge engineers' technical decisions, and to pose questions about technical solutions as seen through the eyes of a customer. Recalling his early days at Vestas, Fritz indicated that Vestas faced a whole range of challenges:

> We had to recognize the fact that the entire world around Vestas and the wind power industry had changed significantly in just a few years. Vestas had not succeeded in making very much progress

during the same period. This meant that Vestas found itself in a position in which three absolutely fundamental premises had altered radically, without the company having changed correspondingly: the market, the customers and the competition. As regards the customers, a completely new and demanding segment had begun to fill the company's order books – that of the large energy companies to which wind power is just another energy source in their portfolio. I, myself, had worked for one of these companies as one of Vestas's customers, so I knew the greater and different demands that were being made with regard to quality, capability, forecasting, delivery reliability and the like. Moreover, with regard to the competition we had moved in just a short space of time into a completely different league, especially after companies such as Siemens and GE had come into the picture. These were companies that had been in the generating business for more than a century, and which were now bringing a serious amount of money and comprehensive know-how into the wind power market. *(Senior Vice-President Robert P. Fritz [*Win(d)*, no. 11, 2008])*

While the projects served to rejuvenate Vestas in the changed competitive environment, two areas in particular were subject to considerable attention: Communication, and people and culture. Part of Engel's plan was to establish a new business unit, People & Culture, as well as to strengthen communication activities related to the company's stakeholders.

Internal and external communication

Vestas learned about the self-reinforcing relationship between internal and external communication the hard way. Following the challenging merger with NEG Micon, employees could read relatively unpleasant news stories based on journalists' speculations. The employees got their information from the media rather than from the company itself, which created negative feelings inside the company. The key to curbing unconstructive gossip was to make the company more transparent. According to Engel, one of management's key tasks was to provide stakeholders with genuine, trustworthy information about the direction and state of the company, regardless of whether this information was positive or negative: "You have to have the guts to stand up and say 'this is what we strive for. This is the way we need to go'. I have to outline the course I navigate by to my 15,000 employees as well … Evidently, it is much more pleasant to tell people good news than bad news. The most important thing, however, is for people to know exactly where we stand. No one expects everything you put forward to be fantastic" (*Berlingske Tidende*, December 30, 2007).

Following his presentation of the new strategy plan in May 2005, Engel visited all of the company's divisions to discuss Vestas's new vision and strategic direction. His primary objective was to ensure that no employee could be in any doubt about management's intentions for the company. According to him, such an objective could only be achieved through frequent, intense communication. Consequently, Vestas decided that quarterly statements should include key financial information, information that was previously only made available twice a year through short memos. Furthermore, each quarter the CEO spoke via webcast (with simultaneous translation into six languages) to all of the company's employees. These presentations always concerned the current state of Vestas. Employee attendance was mandatory. When asked whether the company could afford to stop production for one hour, Engel simply replied: "I believe it is too expensive not to" (Annual Meeting of the Confederation of Danish Industries, September 2007). This form of communication underlined management's commitment to creating a more unified, transparent Vestas.

External communication also saw an appreciable upgrade, most notably in terms of investor relations activities. Normally a company relocates production. Vestas, however, relocated its financial presentations from Denmark to London to obtain stronger media exposure and to allow for interviews with prominent new stations like the BBC, CNN, and Bloomberg. With exposure to 400–500 million potential viewers, this move provided the company with a unique opportunity to propagate messages and knowledge about wind energy.

Diverse people and a shared culture

Part of "The Will to Win" plan was to breed a shared company culture. Creating one Vestas across geographical boundaries and functional lines was seen as a key prerequisite for effective cooperation between units and employees ("The Will to Win," 2005–8). The President of the People & Culture unit, Roald Jakobsen, explained:

> *One Vestas* has to do with building up a shared understanding of our company. It is about creating the best possible conditions for a culture with the emphasis on community and room for the individual. The key to success is primarily rooted in our employees' attitude. And I hope and believe that we will soon reach the milestone where we all recognize that *The Will to Win*, the vision, the mission and our four core values are inextricably linked together as a die-cast foundation for our common journey towards our goal. More than 10,000 colleagues, pulling together in the same direction. *One Vestas. (Vestas Annual Report, 2005)*

The People & Culture unit was responsible for developing and implementing programs for recruitment (such as graduate programs), human resource development, and international cooperation among approximately 14,000 employees from fifty-six nations. The company had seen a heavy increase in employee intake, with the number of employees rising from approximately 10,300 in 2005 to 13,820 in 2007. In 2008, Vestas planned to recruit 2,500 new employees (see Figure 4.3). Hence, there was a great need to integrate and unite new colleagues under the umbrella of Vestas's culture. The key constituents of the company's culture involved an entrepreneurial spirit, a focus on team performance, and the possession of the will and power to execute (see Box 4.3).

A key challenge for People & Culture was to balance diversity and cultural cohesion (or community spirit). Vestas strongly believed that the best results were achieved through diversity and exposure to ideas from all over the world. The company could not solely rely on

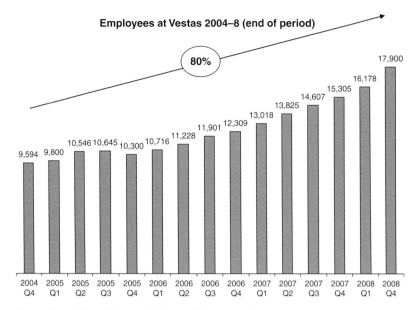

Source: Vestas Financial Quarterly Reports 2004–8. 2005 Q1 and 2008
Q4 are estimated from 2007 Q3 Financial Report

FIGURE 4.3 Expected growth in employee intake

knowledge that emanated from Denmark. Vestas had established a global presence (i.e., R&D and production) to tap knowledge and ideas from multiple locations. It was also able to set up teams with members of different nationalities and diverse backgrounds. Exposure to diversity from the locational and people perspectives was considered key to Vestas's competiveness. For example, the President of Technology R&D, Finn Strøm Madsen, remarked: "It is through technology that we need to differentiate ourselves. Our goal is to have a borderless, global setup with hubs in Europe, Asia and North America. Via this network, we are aiming for an ongoing flow of ideas and technology for developing the best products and services" (*Vestas Magazine Win(d)*, February 2008).

To further support the creation of one Vestas, employee bonus schemes were based on the notion that all employees were part of the same value chain. They would therefore profit if the company performed well. For example, 70 percent of the 2008 bonus pay schemes depend on Vestas's overall performance (i.e., earnings before interest and taxes [EBIT] margin, new working capital, customer loyalty, and market share), while the reminding 30 percent hinge upon efforts of local business units. The way in which incentives and bonus schemes were organized supported Vestas's view that "the whole is greater than the sum of its parts." Excellent results were achieved through the combination of highly skilled individuals on global teams. The bonus schemes had to reflect a sense of common responsibility and belonging to the organization. Drawing on a football analogy, Engel explained: "We at Vestas play as a team for the World Championship every day. We need to function as a team. It does not make sense if you have a fantastic forward who makes five goals in every game but at the same time your goalkeeper lets in six goals" (interview with Ditlev Engel, February 19, 2008).

In 2007, People & Culture launched an initiative to work proactively to develop internal management practices and leadership attitudes. Most of Vestas's middle managers were trained engineers and were not always comfortable with handling challenges when the company was under pressure. Yet, according to Engel, to succeed as a leader one had to be willing to take risks and be exposed. That was how a leader would have an impact. To respond to the management challenge, People & Culture arranged leadership seminars for the top 200 managers and assigned personal coaches to the top 500 managers to develop their leadership skills.

STAGE SHIFT NO. 2: EXTERNAL POSITIONING AND MAKING CHANGES STICK

Vestas's strategy plan worked. The 2007 results showed improved profitability and net working capital, while the third priority – a global market share of at least 35 percent – proved to be too ambitious (see Figure 4.4). The company still enjoyed a comfortable lead over Gamesa and GE Wind. When the 2007 results were released, Vestas downgraded its long-term market share target to 28 percent, which would

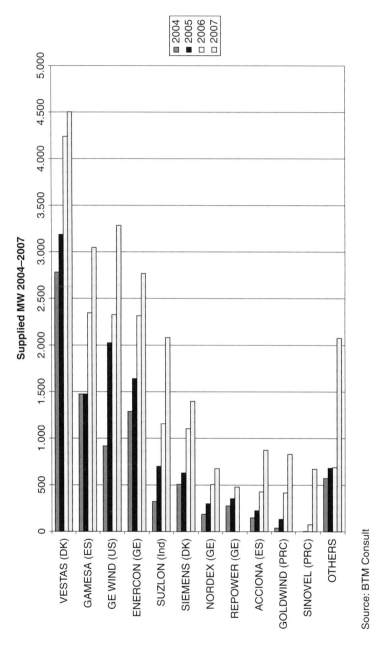

Source: BTM Consult

FIGURE 4.4 Development in market share, 2004–7

still provide it with a notable share of future installed megawatts. The company's projections suggested global wind power penetration to go from 1 percent to at least 10 percent in 2020, or from 75,000 MW to at least 1,000,000 MW. Given this favorable market outlook, Vestas saw an opportunity to position itself as the key player to diffuse messages about wind energy and as the player inclined to bring stakeholders, such as politicians, governments, and citizens, into discussions. Therefore, in the second quarter of 2007, Vestas introduced its "No. 1 in Modern Energy" strategy internally and complemented it with a global marketing campaign to support the message. It stressed that under catchy slogans and wordplays like "CO_2 buster with wings" or "A year's power supply in just two hours?" the "Modern Energy" strategy was more "sticky" and deep-rooted, encompassing an obligation on the behalf of its employees to drive discussions, messages, and trends – not just for Vestas but for the industry as a whole.

Governmental relations

To strengthen Vestas's dialog with politicians, public servants, non-governmental organizations (NGOs) and wind power lobbyists around the world, the company established a department for governmental relations in 2006. Peter C. Brun, formerly the Deputy Manager of the Danish Foreign Ministry's office for Trade & Industry's International Conditions, was appointed to head the department. Brun's main responsibility was to lobby for wind energy to gain as much credit among government decision makers as the fuel and fossil energy companies. As he stated upon his appointment: "The wind turbine manufacturers have spent many years developing technologies that can compete financially with oil and gas. However, the international energy sector is highly politicized sector. Consequently, it is just as important to develop the political competitiveness of wind power. We ourselves have to explain why wind power should have much more weight in energy policy" (Vestas press release, June 1, 2006). His office played a key role in positioning wind power on the global agenda. It provided the right data, as well as information on specific markets and regulatory frameworks, for people to form their understanding of modern energy and then make decisions.

At the beginning of 2008, the governmental relations department had offices in Denmark and the USA, and plans were in place to establish a presence in key markets like China, India, and Spain to strengthen relations with local politicians. The department had experienced an increased interest in wind energy, which resulted in meetings with influential decision makers, including heads of states and deputy ministers from emerging wind power nations. Moreover, meetings with US senators and leading public servants in Washington had made it easier to "enter" the lobbies in Washington and get the message across – people were more willing to listen (interview with Ditlev Engel, February 19, 2008). In fact, Vestas's presence as the only wind turbine maker at the World Economic Forum's Annual Meeting in Davos, Switzerland in 2008, where it aimed to put a focus on the political and financial benefits of wind energy and to influence the debate on the world's future energy choices, was perhaps the most prestigious result of governmental relations efforts.

Stakeholder management included not only parties in the political arena but also universities and educational milieus. In collaboration with Aalborg University, Vestas established a comprehensive research program in 2007. The program included at least ten PhD projects, numerous scholarships for graduate students, and the financing of a five-year professorial tenure. Vestas's aim was to accelerate research and development in the field of components and systems within power electronics for use in the wind turbine industry. Apart from supporting leading research talents in developing specialist competences, the program also created an awareness of career opportunities following completion of a PhD in this field. Similar strategic alliances with educational environments in the USA were planned but not yet publicized. Vestas regarded its presence among leading global education institutions as an important method of advancing and strengthening related research environments, and inspiring internal R&D efforts and their commercialization (Vestas press release, August 29, 2007).

Global information and lobbying campaign

Obtaining a global reach with key messages was expensive. At the presentation of the 2007 results, Vestas announced that it planned to spend more than it ever had before to run advertisements and engage in various sponsorships. Full-page advertisements in the *Wall Street Journal* and sponsorship of CNN programs and *Financial Times* (*FT*) coverage at the World Economic Forum's top meeting in Davos were some of the initial testaments of Vestas's "Modern Energy" campaign. According to the company, the main goals of these initiatives were to push key wind energy messages (or value propositions) into the global scene, make them known, and inspire reflections among readers and viewers. For example, the *FT* sponsorship meant that Vestas was the sole sponsor of two sixteen-page special reports on the Economic Forum. According to Vestas's communication and IR chief, Peter W. Kruse, the sponsorship of the *FT* coverage at Davos 2008 was "an excellent opportunity for Vestas to raise the audience's awareness of wind power as modern energy. We've worked with the FT to design a package with the purpose of bringing the attention of global business and political decision makers to the advantages offered by wind power, a competitive, predictable, independent and clean energy source with a fast ramp-up" (www.brandrepublic.com/News/778507/Wind-power-supplier-sponsors-FT-coverage-Davos/).

Collapsed wind turbines and deteriorated customer satisfaction

While Vestas's economic performance improved after Engel took over as CEO, customer satisfaction worsened. Back in 2005, Engel had pointed to customer satisfaction as a warning sign. In 2000, 96 percent of the company's customers were satisfied, but by 2006 the customer loyalty index was at a mere 48 percent.[1] The main points of critique related to poor accessibility to Vestas employees and long delivery times. The critique centered around Vestas's execution capabilities and, to a lesser extent, the turbines themselves. If customer satisfaction was to support Vestas's efforts to regain market shares, the negative trend needed to be reversed. To combat the poor customer loyalty index, the company made customer satisfaction a key priority in 2008, when it became a central part of the bonus scheme with a customer loyalty index target of sixty (Vestas Annual Report, 2007).

In addition, Vestas struggled with problems with wind turbines that collapsed. A number of incidents at the end of 2007 and the beginning of 2008 in Scotland, England, and Sweden caused skeptical customer organizations in Holland and Germany to raise allegations of arrogant behavior and a lack of responsibility (www.tv2.dk, January 14, 2008). Vestas tightened its safety procedures and stressed that the accidents were isolated. The CEO's message to the employees was crystal clear: "We have experienced a series of accidents the last couple of months. It is simply not good enough. For us, failure is not an option. I am not out to get someone in particular, but we have to ensure that everything is in order. We need to take Vestas to the next level. One accident is not OK, but I will also stress that we do not see a general problem with our wind turbines" (*RB-Børsen*, February 27, 2008, published in *ErhvervsBladet*).

The accidents *per se* could be regarded as a drop in the ocean. The more alarming fact was that runaway turbines, combined with poor customer loyalty, prompted publicity that openly questioned Vestas as a reliable and trustworthy business partner.

Re-examining Vestas's journey over the past three years, the "diamond" appeared more polished. With an operating profit that amounted to €291 million in 2007, the burning platform that had spawned Engel's

---

[1] According to a new calculation method, which gives a customer loyalty index where the average number of delivered MW in the individual business units during the last three years is used to weight the votes (Vestas Annual Report, 2007).

strategy seemed to have vanished. According to Vestas, however, this was far from the case. Extensive pressures to take the wind energy giant to a new and even higher level were evident. The "Will to Win" plan had been internally focused, aimed at fixing the fundamentals, such as improving profitability and reducing net working capital. Communication had been presented as a key management tool for transforming the company into an open, transparent, and communicative organization. Vestas now prepared to restate and expand its global leadership position via the "No. 1 in Modern Energy" campaign, which was launched in the second quarter of 2007. This marked an important shift toward a more external focus. Abandoning humbleness and servility, the idea was to establish a future platform through which Vestas would stage and position itself as a spokesperson for the entire industry.

While this worldwide positioning reinforced internal confidence and commitment, the shift brought challenges as well. It required Vestas to maintain its leadership position over time (its market share fell from 28 percent in 2006 to an estimated 23 percent in 2007). More importantly, Vestas's self-appointed leadership position put the company in the firing line and made it the subject of increased media and industry attention – not only when positive themes needed commenting but also when wind turbines collapsed, customer satisfaction deteriorated, or component shortages challenged growth forecasts. Industry leadership meant exposure, both good and bad, and highlighted the need to alleviate compromising questions and to stay steady in choppy waters.

Moreover, the Modern Energy platform implied a mindset change for Vestas's employees and stakeholders, a need to inculcate the image of a modern, "next generation" wind maker. How could the company ensure that its own employees and stakeholders would compare it to dynamic, fast-growing, flexible companies, such as those in the IT industry, rather than to more traditional industrial companies? How could it change the perception and mindset of its employees, politicians, and governments? The fact that it had to work with complex physical structures and pieces weighing 250 tons, which were difficult to ramp up quickly, only complicated the challenge. Putting Modern Energy at the top of the agenda was the initial step. Crafting and communicating the messages, both internally and externally, and then executing within this new staged business platform required a real shift in mindsets and culture.

VESTAS: SUMMARY AND QUESTIONS FOR DISCUSSION

Vestas is a significant example of the rise of a new industry and how the shift from the grass-roots sector to a highly competitive global business environment paved the way for management innovation. Whereas Vestas previously was driven by a mix of romantic commitment and local support, it was recently transformed into a global business that competes based on visionary aspirations, professionalism, and the ability to engage internal and external stakeholders. It was founded by local entrepreneurs supported by political goodwill and subsidies in the wake of a growing awareness of alternative energy. It survived a financial collapse and started its global journey after a merger with a Danish competitor. Rising oil prices, global environmental concerns about future energy, and a political aspiration to reduce dependencies on oil and gas have turned the wind industry into a huge market, where Vestas has a leading position. However, the company is confronted with fierce competition not only in relation to technology and operational excellence but also in terms of the ability to engage politicians and large customers. Thus, it has been forced to innovate its ways of working in numerous areas, spearheaded by a young and highly ambitious CEO, who from day one stated the company's global aspirations. He made several highly symbolic gestures, such as presenting the Annual Report from London and being interviewed by BBC/CNN before the local Danish media, making it clear that Vestas was seeking to innovate itself in ways that matched the global origin of its customers and increasingly also of its employees.

It has not all been a bed of roses. Vestas is still struggling with declining customer satisfaction, while its competitors are catching up in terms of technology and customer relations. Also, there is a growing resistance in some markets concerning the environmental impact of the mega wind turbines. However, following the BP oil disaster in the USA in 2010, one must expect an even stronger push toward the replacement of oil with other sources of energy. Only time will tell if Vestas will be able to leverage its current position and reputation in the marketplace and continue to grow. As such, the case facilitates discussion of the following issues:

1. What were the most significant management innovations undertaken by Engel and his team in Vestas?
   a. How did the company rethink its strategic goal-setting?
   b. How did it change its internal governance structure? How was this structure linked to its goal-setting?
   c. How did it create operational excellence? How did it introduce new ways of working?
   d. How did globalization influence its people management and internal/external communication practices?
2. In Vestas a wide range of related organizational innovations were developed in order to create a stronger alignment with internal and external stakeholders. As part of envisioning and communicating these innovations, the CEO used metaphors from the political system, such as government and ministers. In addition, the goal-setting of the company, e.g., wind, oil, and gas, had an overall political aspiration.
   a. How can the use of metaphors help top management envision and communicate management innovations?
   b. What are the differences between business and governments as management systems?
   c. How relevant is the political metaphor in the energy industry?
3. As part of its transformation, Vestas has been on a journey from a local industrial manufacturer to a global fast-growing hi-tech/gazelle-type company.
   a. Which innovations in particular marked the transformation into a global player?

4. Looking at the future development of wind energy on a global scale, which areas of management innovation are envisioned for Vestas in the future?

   a. What are the most critical barriers for continuous high growth in the future for Vestas?

   b. How should Vestas overcome these barriers?

ADDITIONAL SOURCES IN RELATION TO VESTAS

www.vestas.com

Pedersen, T. and Larsen, M. M. (2009). *Vestas Wind Systems A/S – Exploiting Global R&D Synenergies*. Ivey Publishing, Case. 9B09M079.

5   Coloplast: Innovating innovation

"Global Research and Development (R&D) has joint responsibility with Global Marketing for the development of new products. The products need to be developed at a much higher pace. That is why we start applying all possible LEAN-methods in order to reduce the time it takes to bring new products to the market."

CCO Lars Rasmussen in *World of Coloplast*, No. 1, January 2008

As he presented the company's guidance for the coming quarters, Coloplast's President and CEO, Sten Scheibye, felt an incipient pessimism among the equity analysts as they posed critical questions. Flanked by CCO Lars Rasmussen and CFO Lene Skole, he had already gone through the company's full-year financial statement for 2006/7. Now the corps of equity analysts was puzzled about the company's long-term targets, which had been the subject of varying statements in recent years. While recognizing the need for clarity, the critique that Coloplast had become less transparent did not affect Scheibye. According to him, the company's underlying performance for 2006/7 was satisfactory, with revenue growth of 20 percent and substantial profitability gains resulting from the ongoing relocation of production to Hungary and China (see Table 5.1). Commenting on the full-year financial statement, the CEO noted: "Our financial statement was not well-received ... I understand why they are questioning our forecasts. Yet, I do not grasp their pessimism. It is not a downgrading" (*Jyllands-Posten*, November 22, 2007).

In reality, Sten Scheibye was more concerned with the concrete means of realizing the outlined targets. In that respect, 2007 had been a very eventful and dramatic year. Coloplast was in the middle of a transformation. Originally a Danish company mainly operating in Europe, it was now becoming a truly global company with value

Table 5.1 *Five years of key figures and ratios*

	2006/7	2005/6	2004/5	2003/4	2002/3
Income statement (DKK million)					
Revenue	8,042	6,709	6,232	6,069	5,610
R&D costs	319	244	215	202	168
EBITDA	1,590	1,304	1,348	1,295	1,195
Operating profit before special items	1,061	939	1,026	988	909
EBIT	749	879	1,000	988	909
Net financial income and expense	–154	–222	–163	–89	–21
Profit before tax	595	657	837	899	889
Coloplast's share of profit for the year	837	614	553	577	567
Revenue growth (%)					
Annual growth in revenue	20	8	8	8	1
Components of the increase (% growth from year to year)					
Organic growth	10	8	8	10	11
Currency effect	–2	1	0	–2	–5
Acquired businesses	12	7	0	0	0
Divested businesses	0	–8	0	0	–5
Cash flows and investments (DKK million)					
Cash flow from operating activities	1,064	991	1,353	845	911
Cash flow from investing activities	35	–3,018	–434	–621	–783
Acquisition of property, plant and equipment (gross)	745	415	399	544	578
Cash flow from financing activities	–1,423	782	–446	–239	307
Free cash flow	1,099	–2,027	919	224	128

Table 5.1 (*cont.*)

	2006/7	2005/6	2004/5	2003/4	2002/3
Key ratios					
Operating margin, EBIT (%)	9	13	16	16	16
Operating margin, EBITDA (%)	20	19	22	21	21
Return on average invested capital (ROAIC) (%)	10	15	18	17	17
Economic profit (DKK million)	−227	349	279	221	213
Return on equity (%)	30	23	23	27	32
Average number of FTEs	7.063	5.437	6.159	6.085	5.774
Revenue per FTE (DKK million)	1.14	1.23	1.01	0.99	0.97

Source: Coloplast annual reports

chain functions scattered all over the world and a growing position as a global market leader. While the relocation of production was well underway, other areas, such as R&D, sales, and marketing, were on the threshold of becoming more standardized and global. During the previous spring, following comprehensive analytical work, Coloplast launched the biggest organizational restructuring in a quarter of a century, which affected most of the company's employees, product divisions, and business areas (see Figures 5.1 and 5.2). These multiple, pervasive changes needed time to settle. "This is the largest change introduced to the company in the last 23 years. We need to break radically with the way we organize our work and processes if our growth ambitions are to be realized" (CCO Lars Rasmussen, *Berlingske Tidende*, February 22, 2007).

Two changes were particularly sensational. First, Coloplast's commercial success had been achieved through incremental innovation (introducing small-step improvements to existing product successes) and, to a lesser extent, from groundbreaking, commercially attractive yet more risky inventions. The new organizational setup aimed to establish the necessary foundation and competences to

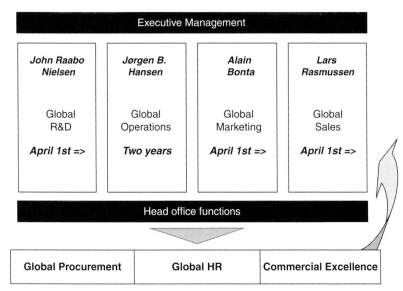

Source: Coloplast annual reports

FIGURE 5.1 Functionally divided organization, spring 2007

embrace both incremental and radical innovations. The product process, from idea to market, was streamlined and products were to be
based on customer pull. Second, due to the restructuring and consolidation of various sales regions, as well as the creation of a commercial
excellence function, sales staff would be able to spend more time with
the right customers, develop stronger relationships, and gain better
access to support tools and training. The task for the commercial
excellence function was to challenge targets and set standards for the
sales divisions, monitor their performance carefully, and define and
ensure that best practices were diffused. Commercial excellence
worked as a support function aimed at professionalizing Coloplast's
approach to selling.

Pivotal questions regarding the extent to which these organizational changes would materialize – and how they would benefit
Coloplast's businesses – remained. As Scheibye considered how to
reap the benefits of the shift in organizational structure from matrix

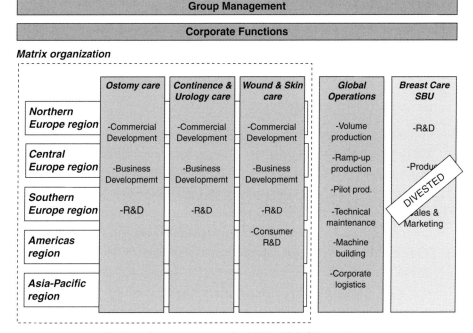

FIGURE 5.2 Divisional structure since the 1980s, Global Operations as introduced in 2005

to functional lines, his thoughts focused on such critical aspects as standardization, creativity, and the R&D mindset:

1. Generally, a main objective of the reshuffle was to accelerate Coloplast's innovation pace and boost sales through increased standardization. Standardization within global operations had shown remarkable results. Could the same mechanisms be transferred to sales, marketing, and R&D without compromising creativity?

2. A more specific theme involved the company's R&D capabilities. Coloplast had a long, solid track record of internal innovations. However, recent attempts to bring external innovation inside had prompted a mindset change, although this change was only grudgingly made in some cases. Would the new setup allow the company to tap into and utilize the value-creating ideas of its employees and those of other parties beyond its boundaries? Would the company's R&D employees learn to appreciate the

possibility that ideas from external environments could enrich and inspire internal research, thereby avoiding the "not invented here" syndrome?

Hopefully, 2008 would provide some answers to these important issues.

INTRODUCING COLOPLAST

Coloplast's story begins in 1954 with Elise Sørensen and her sister, Thora, who underwent an ostomy surgery. As a nurse, Elise wanted to help her sister. To do so, she developed a disposable ostomy[1] bag made from polyethylene that could adhere directly to the skin around the stoma.[2] She met with a number of plastic manufacturers to put her idea into production, but none of them saw the business potential of the idea. Among these plastic manufacturers was Aage Louis-Hansen at Dansk Plastic Emballage, who only agreed to operationalize the device after having been convinced by his wife. This decision laid the foundation of Coloplast. The world's first disposable ostomy bag was produced in 1955 and Coloplast was founded in 1957. Today, the company's mission is to be "the preferred source of medical devices and associated services contributing to a better quality of life" (www. coloplast.com; see Figure 5.3 for Coloplast's milestones).

Coloplast specializes in three business areas (see Figure 5.4 and Table 5.2). Products from the ostomy, urology, and continence division are targeted at people whose intestinal outlet has been surgically rerouted through the abdominal wall, as well as at people having problems controlling their bladder or bowel movements. The wound and skin care division offers a variety of dressings to treat difficult-to-heal wounds, active dressings that reduce pain in chronic wounds, and

---

[1] The word "ostomy" refers to the type of surgery required when a person has lost the normal function of the bowel or the bladder. The surgery falls into three general categories: *colostomy* (diverting the large intestine), *ileostomy* (diverting the small intestine), and *urostomy* (diverting the passage of urine) (www.coloplast.com).

[2] When someone undergoes ostomy surgery, the surgeon creates a "stoma," or surgical opening, through the abdominal wall. Bodily wastes can then be expelled into a special appliance attached to the stoma – the kinds of appliances Coloplast makes. A stoma can be temporary or permanent (www.coloplast.com).

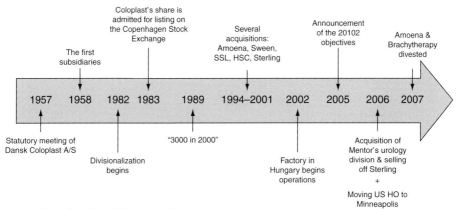

Source: Coloplast financial presentation

FIGURE 5.3 Historical timeline and milestones

antifungal creams, lotions, cleansers, and moisturizers to support the natural processes of the skin. Coloplast also had a breast care division until 2007, when it was divested to the German investment company, Granville Baird, for DKK 762 million.

A hallmark of Coloplast's identity has been its ability to listen and respond to the needs of nurses and end-users. Some say that this ability constituted a key competitive advantage for the company. When it celebrated its fiftieth anniversary, more than 6,000 meetings were organized between employees and persons who use a Coloplast product. The idea was to give every employee an opportunity to hear end-users tell their story about their daily life, experiences, and challenges.

Historically, ostomy care had been Coloplast's *raison d'être*. However, the acquisition of the urology division of US-based Mentor in 2006 marked a shift in strategic direction and extended the product range to include invasive products. The acquisition also provided a platform to expand in the US market. Coloplast needed to get accustomed to a fundamental new business model that was characterized by low-volume, high-value, cyclical movements, higher product launch

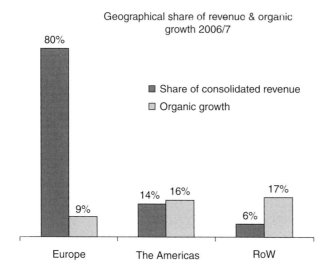

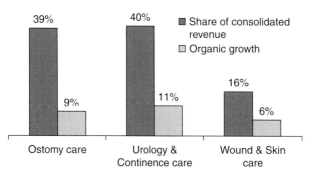

FIGURE 5.4 Geographical and business areas, organic growth, 2006/7

frequency, increased attention to clinical evidence and regulatory demands, and surgeons as key stakeholders. Continence and urology care represented 40 percent of the company's consolidated revenue in 2006/7, which put it on a level similar to ostomy care, which still constituted a key business area. However, the latter's future prospects appeared less auspicious (see Figure 5.4 and Table 5.2).

Table 5.2 *Financial results, market value, and Coloplast shares*

	Ostomy care		Urology and continence care		Wound and skin care	
	2006/7	2005/6	2006/7	2005/6	2006/7	2005/6
Gross revenue (DKK million)	3,107	2,867	3,199	2,233	1,269	1,223
Organic growth	9%	7%	11%	14%	6%	6%
Share of consolidated revenue	39%	43%	40%	33%	16%	18%
Global market value (DKK billion)	9.6	9.3	17.0	14.5	13.3	12.6
Global market growth	3–5%	1–3%	8–10%	7%	5%	7%
Coloplast's global market share	32%	31%	19%	15%	10%	10%

Source: Coloplast financial presentations

STRATEGIC OUTLOOK

During the financial statement conference call in 2007, long-term financial targets were updated. The year 2012 was abandoned as a benchmark and the long-term targets were set as: 1) A doubling of economic profit[3] at least every five years; 2) organic sales growth of approximately 10 percent per annum; and 3) EBIT of 18–20 percent.

To realize these ambitious growth targets, Coloplast outlined a number of strategic initiatives involving such aspects as an accelerated

---

[3] *Economic profit* can be defined as the difference between the revenue received from the sale of an output and the opportunity cost of the inputs used. In calculating economic profit, opportunity costs are deducted from revenues earned. Opportunity costs are the alternative returns foregone by using the chosen inputs. As a result, you can have a significant accounting profit with little to no economic profit.

innovation rate, a process to streamline time to market, and the introduction of new products on a global scale. To fund these growth
initiatives, the company relied on four pillars, of which the setup of a
Global Operations function in 2005 had been the most comprehensive
and had delivered promising results (see Figure 5.5 for a full overview of
strategic priorities and funding initiatives). The goals of Global
Operations were to ease the relocation of production to Hungary and
China, to define common standards for all factories and key processes,
to establish world-class manufacturing, to reap productivity gains, and
to enjoy the benefits of a lower cost base. As part of this plan, production facilities in Denmark were to be consolidated from six to three,
while new factories would be built in Hungary and China. In addition,
machinery was to be built in China. The procedure was quite extensive
as, by 2012, approximately 70 percent of Coloplast's products would be
produced in Hungary and China, compared with 25–30 percent in 2007
(see Figure 5.6 for Coloplast's worldwide presence).

Although the relocation efforts had already yielded substantial
productivity improvements, Coloplast expected to see the full effects
of productivity gains, the lower cost base, and synergies in the 2008/9
results.

Healthcare reforms and tenders squeezing profit margins

The fact that European and US health authorities planned to introduce
tenders or redefined reimbursement schemes constituted a serious
threat to Coloplast's future bottom line. The German decision to
reduce reimbursements on ostomy products by 13 percent on January
1, 2005 negatively affected Coloplast's sales by DKK 150 million given
the company's heavy presence in this market (15–20 percent of revenue). On January 1, 2007, German reimbursement rates for continence products were lowered by 10 percent. At the same time, the
introduction of competitive bidding rounds by the German healthcare
authorities threatened to lower future revenue growth and earnings.
However, perhaps the most severe challenge was a goodwill write-
down of DKK 283 million in one of Coloplast's German distributional

Investing in innovation & growth through:

- **Key player strategy/NPD.** Continue the successful key player/NPD strategy at the hospitals

- **Increased innovation rate.** The value of the new product pipeline must grow 50% more than Coloplast's revenue

- **FIGARO*.** Optimize time to market and global roll-out of new products

- **RACE**.** Support the NPD (hospital) strategy with retention and conversion activities in the community

- **New markets.** Invest in new and emerging markets to secure long-term growth

- **M&A.** Improve ability to identify, acquire, and integrate new businesses

*From Innovation to Global Accelerated Roll-Out

**Retention and Conversion Excellence

Financing growth through:

- **Global Operations.** Reduced time to market and low-cost manufacturing setup

- **Lean/abc*.** Continue to roll-out abc to the whole organization to make continous improvements part of the daily business

- **Corporate Procurement.** Establish a corporate procurement function to leverage and professionalize Coloplast corporate wide procurement volumes, processes and skills

- **Shared Service Centers.** Consolidate and unite service functions in order to optimize service and efficiency at a global level

*Acronym for "a better company"

Source: Coloplast financial presentation

FIGURE 5.5 Coloplast's strategic priorities for 2012

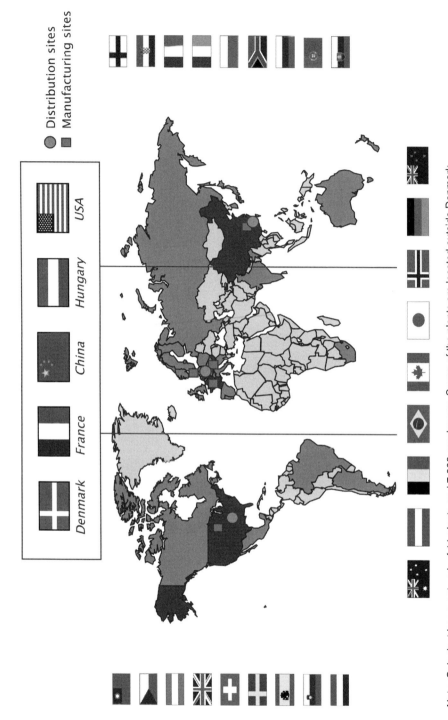

Note: Coloplast has a network of 11 plants and 7,000 employees. Seven of the plants are located outside Denmark.
Source: Coloplast internal documents

FIGURE 5.6 Coloplast's worldwide presence

homecare units, HSC, in 2006/7. This significant write-down was a direct consequence of a high number of employees (nurses) leaving the company, as well as the departure of the former head of HSC to start a competitive business, HomeCare Deutschland.

Similar initiatives were in the making in the UK. Having completed its hearings, the UK Department of Health was expected to announce overall reductions in reimbursements of 10–15 percent for ostomy, urology, and continence care products during 2008. If this proved correct, analysts estimated that Coloplast would lose revenues of DKK 100–150 million per year according to various estimates (i.e., Kaupthing Bank equity research, November 21, 2007). In France, Spain, and Italy – all key markets for Coloplast – preliminary steps had been taken to reduce medical spending and similar initiatives could not be ruled out.

Deliberate responses to ward off the consequences of healthcare reforms were necessary. Apart from seeking operational excellence internally, these developments prompted Coloplast to respond on two fronts. First, it actively prepared tender bids that highlighted the additional services and benefits that were not paid for by the patient. Moreover, the focus was on new, innovative products, as these were often more cost-effective than older, simpler products and enjoyed higher reimbursement rates. Second, the medical devices industry increasingly began to consider clinical efficacy and health economics, as was common in the pharmaceutical industry. For example, in the USA, Coloplast used clinical evidence to support efforts to improve reimbursement for intermittent catheters. By engaging experts from the academic community and compiling health economic analyses, it aimed to provide convincing proof of the cost-effectiveness of innovative products. Moreover, the company set up a market access team within Global Marketing to coordinate reimbursement, pricing, and health economics across countries to ensure the use of best practice.

American footprints

One of the key elements of the strategy involved accelerating business in the USA. The company's previous US endeavors included the acquisition of Sween in 1996 (wound and skin care) and Sterling Medical in 1998 (a specialized distributor of wound care, ostomy, continence, and diabetes products). These did not give it the foothold in the USA it had expected. Although its organic growth in the USA showed positive trends, the market still held tremendous growth opportunities, as exemplified by the continence and urology market. This global market was valued at DKK 17 billion and had annual growth rates of 8–10 percent. The majority of that value was to be found in the USA. By comparison, ostomy care, which had traditionally been Coloplast's key business area, represented an estimated global market value of DKK 10 billion and was more mature, with annual growth rates of 3–5 percent (Annual Report, 2006/7) (see Table 5.2). With the takeover of Mentor, the path was made for a breakthrough in the USA. As one analyst stated: "The acquisition makes them less dependent on growth within the ostomy care segment. The underlying market growth within urology and continence is far more attractive than growth prospects within ostomy care" (Martin Parkhøi, *Berlingske Tidende*, May 19, 2006).

The long-term goal was to reach revenue levels similar to those seen among Coloplast's European operations. Following the DKK 2.9 billion acquisition of Mentor (the biggest in Coloplast's history), the company was the market leader in the lucrative US market for urology products. Moreover, the company established a platform from which it could grow both organically and through acquisitions. The challenge was to balance the continuous search for acquisitions objects with the aspiration of improving earnings, which had been unsatisfactory when compared to European levels. To add credence to the US project, CCO Lars Rasmussen moved to Minneapolis, the site of the company's new North American headquarters. Commenting on the company's US plans, he stated: "We see significant potential for further acquisitions in the US, having completed the integration of Mentor. In principle, acquisition opportunities exist within all of our business areas, but one must understand that it is not like a supermarket. There are a lot of empty shelves and what is out there, in many instances, does not capture our attention" (*Berlingske Tidende*, January 7, 2008).

Perhaps most importantly, through the acquisition of Mentor, Coloplast gained a corps of 200 salesmen. Although this corps would not be selling ostomy, wound, and skin care products, CEO Sten Scheibye believed that its exposure would prompt positive spillover effects in the company's other business areas. In his words, "our significant presence in the urology market should facilitate knowledge and familiarity with other products and thus help us to be considered when large purchase agreements are signed" (*Børsen*, March 29, 2006).

A global mindset

From the outset, the company had an international orientation. In 1957, every second ostomy bag was exported. Today, more than 97 percent of the company's revenue is generated outside of Denmark, although the company still has a strong European focus. In 2006/7, 80 percent of revenue was derived from Europe and another 14 percent was from the Americas, while revenue in emerging market economies, including Asia, constituted a mere 6 percent (Annual Report, 2006/7).

The revitalized US agenda served as further evidence of Coloplast's global aspirations. However, to translate promising aspirations into concrete actions and execution, beliefs needed to be solidified: "Our biggest challenge is that we are a very European organization in terms of mindset and orientation. We do not have the market share that we deserve in the US. Coloplast's future growth needs, to a large degree, to be driven by the American market. This is why we need to accelerate business in the US" (CCO Lars Rasmussen, *Berlingske Tidende*, January 7, 2008).

RESHUFFLING THE ORGANIZATION

In March 2007, Coloplast changed its organizational structure from a matrix to a functional setup. The company was divided into four global units: Marketing, R&D, sales, and operations (see Figure 5.1). The latter was established in 2005 to coordinate and support production. Marketing, R&D, and the three largest markets (the UK, Germany, and France) within global sales reported directly to the CCO, Lars

Rasmussen. Operations reported directly to the CEO. Moreover, a commercial excellence function was established, which was rooted in the company's head office organization but which was exceedingly global in orientation and operations. Thus, the major organizational changes could be seen as responses to the company's aspirations of becoming more global: "It [organizational change] has to do with our intent over the years to adapt Coloplast to a globalized environment. Five years ago, we were a European company with Danish production facilities. This is no longer true" (Sten Scheibye, *Berlingske Tidende*, January 2, 2008).

This was by no means the first time that Coloplast made significant structural adjustments to its organization. For various reasons, the company had "flirted" with both matrix and functional divisions over the course of the previous five years. In general, organizational reshuffles were difficult to implement without significant costs. Every time changes were made, employees needed to re-adapt to their own position, role, and responsibilities. Moreover, energy drainage and stalled momentum constituted plausible risk factors due to uncertainties about the future.

In 2003, the wound care division was spun off into a specialized unit to receive more attention. In the matrix setup, scarce resources were allocated to areas where returns appeared most promising, which in turn undermined other business areas such as wound care (see Figure 5.2). In the fall of 2005, Coloplast announced a new global matrix organization that aimed to "strengthen the company's capabilities for utilizing the market opportunities" and "to create a global platform for future growth and reap the benefits of a larger organization" (www.coloplast.com). The wound care and skin health businesses were merged into the wound and skin care division, comprising the third pillar in the global matrix organization on a par with ostomy and continence care. Local sales and marketing was handled by Coloplast's subsidiaries, while the divisions were responsible for strategic marketing, product launch support, and R&D. Only breast care continued as an independent business unit, as its customers, distribution channels, and technologies were distinct (breast care was divested in 2007).

The reshuffle in 2007 was motivated by an increased focus on boosting sales and accelerating Coloplast's innovation rate. Moreover, it was an attempt to streamline and standardize business processes and to fortify best practice development and dissemination: "Our competitive position and growth possibilities not only depend on our profitability, but also to a great extent on our ability to innovate as well as on the strength of customer relations. We have therefore analyzed our activities in the areas of innovation, sales and marketing and the conclusion was that we will implement a new organizational structure aimed at accelerating growth" (Coloplast press release, published in *Jyllands-Posten*, February 22, 2007).

The new functional setup could also be seen as an attempt to accelerate the diffusion of standardization and lean principles in Coloplast. While engineers in production were thrilled with the lean philosophy, it was more difficult for sales and marketing professionals to grow accustomed to the lean principles and tools. According to Scheibye, these staff members would have to be convinced that selling was not an art but was hard repetitive work based on a systematic, fact-based approach: "The changes we have set in motion are, to some extent, very pervasive and necessitate some cultural adaptation and in some instances even new management" (presentation given at CBS, February 6, 2008).

Reactions in local subsidiaries were mixed, as less positive voices pointed to the limited room for maneuver. Local kingdoms faced dissolution. Scheibye stated that it was still too early to assess the eventual effects of the organizational changes. Still, according to various internal process parameters, the prospects were auspicious. The change was expected to have a positive impact on results in 2008 (*Børsen*, August 16, 2007).

Commercial excellence: Building a world-class organization

Influenced by recommendations from consultancies and inspired by other large Danish companies, such as A.P. Møller, Carlsberg, and companies in the pharma industry, Coloplast established a commercial excellence function as part of the reshuffle. The function was composed of two units: A "sales and marketing task force," whose primary tasks involved design, implementation, and support of sales and marketing programs in Coloplast subsidiaries; and a "business and performance management" unit, which set targets and monitored them closely through monthly reviews with subsidiary management (see Figure 5.7). Building its *raison d'être* on analytical, design, and implementation capabilities, the commercial excellence team was composed, in part, of employees who were analytical- or logical-reasoning types, and of "bridge builders" with an extensive network throughout Coloplast's subsidiaries. The latter were a pivotal resource for securing local buy-ins on defined projects. The commercial excellence unit was regarded internally as a "talent factory" in which employees could develop their leadership skills. As of March 2008, the commercial excellence unit was still firming up project ideas and recruitment.

The first step for the sales and marketing task force was to conduct an assessment survey in which each subsidiary had to describe project needs in terms of professionalizing sales and marketing competences, and then prioritize these needs accordingly. Subsequently, three aggregated themes were defined: 1) Sales, 2) marketing and 3) pricing. France and England were selected as pilot countries. In cooperation with the Boston Consulting Group (BCG) and with the involvement of local management, the sales and marketing unit ran two concurrent sales excellence projects. The project group developed a standardized model for improving segmentation and targeting. In practice, the project was concerned with identifying those customers that were worth more time being spent on them. The next step was to improve sales quality, but a final implementation decision had not yet been taken. Project progress was monitored through status meetings via well-defined key performance indicators (KPIs). Initial results were promising and further roll-outs in additional subsidiaries were planned.

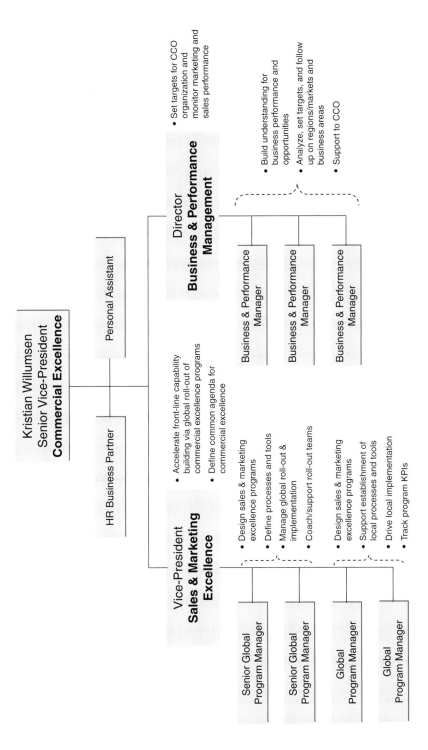

Kristian Willumsen
Senior Vice-President
Commercial Excellence

Personal Assistant

HR Business Partner

Vice-President
**Sales & Marketing
Excellence**

- Accelerate front-line capability building via global roll-out of commercial excellence programs
- Define common agenda for commercial excellence

Director
**Business & Performance
Management**

- Set targets for CCO organization and monitor marketing and sales performance

- Build understanding for business performance and opportunities
- Analyze, set targets, and follow up on regions/markets and business areas
- Support to CCO

Business & Performance Manager

Business & Performance Manager

Business & Performance Manager

Senior Global Program Manager

- Design sales & marketing excellence programs
- Define processes and tools
- Manage global roll-out & implementation
- Coach/support roll-out teams

Senior Global Program Manager

Global Program Manager

- Design sales & marketing excellence programs
- Support establishment of local processes and tools
- Drive local implementation
- Track program KPIs

Global Program Manager

Source: Coloplast internal documents

FIGURE 5.7 Organizational structure of the commercial excellence function

The efforts of the commercial excellence unit, together with the work of the corporate finance unit, substantially improved the way in which Coloplast worked with business reporting. Previously, subsidiaries reported to headquarters using different templates, which made cross-country comparisons difficult. These templates and processes were in the process of being redefined and standardized to include monthly reviews in which CCO Lars Rasmussen participated. This helped him to closely monitor the commercial side of Coloplast's operations. At these sessions, action and improvement areas were identified based on quantitative analysis of sales data: "It appears that systematic reporting and structured follow-up meetings between corporate and the sales regions furthers new ideas more quickly and, in addition, encourages swifter reactions to eventual problem areas" (interview with Senior Global Program Manager Nils Bundgaard, Commercial Excellence, January 24, 2008).

Initial resistance: Communication as mediation

Despite solid results and good feedback from the subsidiaries, the launch of the commercial excellence idea was somewhat difficult. There was a common perception that the commercial excellence team was an extension of headquarters designed to enforce the rules of conduct. Management was aware of this apprehension pitfall and sought to neutralize it by promoting commercial excellence as a supporting, "partner in growth" and dialog-based business unit via a plethora of communication activities including Intranet, informational meetings, and an advisory board including representatives from various sales units. The initial internal assessment exercise also emphasized an open and supportive approach.

In the case of France, Coloplast teamed up with the recently appointed general manager, who was very enthusiastic about implementing sales excellence. His approval and backing helped to convince a number of sales directors and team leaders, but the positive reaction came only after four months of comprehensive meetings in which roles, responsibilities, and interfaces were discussed. To gain acceptance, Coloplast sought to infuse an "ambassador" line of thinking, in which a convinced leader would do his or her best to promote the idea among his or her employees.

With the commercial excellence programs, Coloplast had taken the first step toward becoming a more responsive, less bureaucratized organization. The idea was to accumulate impulses from local subsidiaries and translate these into concrete projects. The plan was to further strengthen collaboration between performance management and the sales and marketing unit through commercial excellence. Business issues identified through the monthly business reviews would occasionally require immediate action or larger projects, which sales and marketing excellence typically would help to scope and implement. Moreover, it was hoped that as subsidiaries became increasingly aware of the benefits of commercial excellence, they would proactively request assistance and support in implementing local projects.

Embracing innovation

Innovation had always been a running theme and a hallmark of Coloplast's philosophy and strategy. Therefore, it was not surprising when the company launched its 2012 strategy and pinpointed innovation leadership as key to realizing the ambitious objectives: 1) 20 percent of revenues to stem from products less than four years old; 2) triple the value of the new product pipeline; and 3) double the speed of innovation. In addition to serving as internal goal indicators, these objectives also served as a strong promise to the company's customers. Moreover, the level of R&D ambition pointed to a pivotal fact – it was not self-evident that the objectives should be accomplished exclusively via Coloplast's own means.

The functional organization was seen as the most adequate setup, strengthening Coloplast's innovative capabilities and accelerating the speed of innovation. Perhaps more interestingly, the organizational reshuffle infused new approaches to R&D on the physiological/mental level as well. It was commonly believed that the chance of success was considerably higher if innovation occurred internally. However, according to management, it was not logical for Coloplast to strive for excellence in everything. The company needed to define its core R&D competences, one of which was design. Management's attempt to cultivate a more open approach to innovation triggered, in some instances, the "not invented here" syndrome among Coloplast's R&D professionals. However, the key point was that external or open innovation did not serve as a substitute for inherent R&D capabilities, but complemented and enriched them. As such, Coloplast's future innovation accomplishments would still be based on its unique accumulated experiences within user-driven innovation, but it was hoped that the new R&D setup would improve the company's ability to source and commercialize external innovation (see Box 5.1 for Coloplast's innovation efforts within the wound care market).

In many ways, the Mentor acquisition served as an eye-opener with respect to innovation pace and the ability to commercialize external innovation. First, 50 percent of Mentor's innovations were driven by external companies. Second, Mentor operated with specific dates for product launches, which called for an extraordinary commitment to the project in question. In comparison, Coloplast planned by the quarter. Third, Mentor challenged Coloplast's innovation process. Over time, employees had developed an exorbitant respect for quality procedures, which had hampered innovation in some cases. For Mentor, this was like a straitjacket. Evidently, some innovation processes contained mandatory quality control aspects, but if Coloplast wanted to accelerate the speed of innovation, flexibility was needed as long as deliberated arguments could support it.

Coloplast moved toward a more open approach that embraced external innovation efforts and fortified collaborative links between R&D and Global Marketing. In the process, key internal technological competences were mapped in technology plans where R&D professionals set the direction, defined R&D programs, and assessed core competences. In fact, Coloplast had declared an objective of including external "content" in its core competences. It was by no means given

BOX 5.1 **Coloplast's innovation in the wound care market**

Coloplast's historical development in the wound care market illustrated in all plainness the company's challenge with regards to radical innovation. Equity analysts and the business media in general had been disappointed with Coloplast's development within wound care for a long time. Specialized in moist wound healing, Coloplast's global market share was a mere 7 percent. In a market valued at DKK 11.2 billion and with 6–7 percent growth rates, the market outlook was positive. However, Coloplast struggled to gain a foothold in the market. In 2006/7, the company grew by an unsatisfactory 6 percent. The market was driven by frequent (new) product introductions, which rapidly became run-of-the-mill items. Thus, the critical parameter to attaining growth was to launch innovative product solutions with high frequency to defend market shares. In the USA, for instance, Coloplast felt the implications of these market dynamics. Following Coloplast's introduction of its antibacterial, silver foam dressing, Contreet, numerous contender products inundated the market, diluting Coloplast's growth.

More recently, Coloplast launched Biatain Ibu, "an active dressing that reduces pain in chronic wounds as well as manages the fluid that exudes from the wound," which according to the company suggested a new paradigm within wound healing as it was "the first dressing ever to combine a highly absorbent foam with local release of ibuprofen" (www.coloplast.com). However, market reactions were less enthusiastic. Sales of Biatain Ibu were slower than expected as "it has proven more demanding than expected to cultivate a market for a new wound care product. But the good news is that it has positive spin-off effects on our additional products" (CEO Sten Scheibye, 2006/7 financial year announcement).

Wound care had been Coloplast's Achilles' heel. The business media had often speculated in divestment. When Mölnlycke, a key competitor, was sold in 2005 to a private equity fund, Coloplast appeared interested, but heavy interest from several private equity funds and industrial players caused the price to skyrocket. Whether Coloplast would become as successful in wound care as in other business areas

BOX 5.1 (CONTINUED)

hinged upon internal capabilities to grow organically and to identify and acquire key niche players with fast-growing technologies. One missed acquisition opportunity was apparently not enough to shatter CEO Sten Scheibye's optimism: "Opportunities definitely exist. We would like to position ourselves well primarily towards the wound & skin care as well as urology and continence segments. Within ostomy care, no obvious opportunities exist. Yet regarding the latter, a fair amount of possibilities exist to buy projects, products, market shares and companies. They do not necessarily have to be large companies. They could be start-ups with interesting technology that may feed and enrich our R&D. This also extends to listed or unlisted corporations or divisions of these" (*Berlingske Tidende*, February 12, 2007).

In order to succeed, Coloplast would have to keep an eye on potential acquisition targets. For instance, in the fastest growing market – active wound healing – Kinetic Concepts had a 95 percent market share, which inhibited potential acquisitions (*Børsen*, June 22, 2007). The company was a relatively new player but had become the overall advanced wound care market leader based on its VAC (Vacuum Assisted Closure) therapy technology. The VAC technology is a controlled application of sub-atmospheric pressure to a wound using a therapy unit to intermittently or continuously convey negative pressure to a specialized wound dressing to help promote wound healing. From 2002 to 2006, revenue from VAC-related technologies increased by 241 percent from US$313.4 million to US$1.07 billion. To make matters worse, Coloplast had actually explored opportunities to introduce a similar technology to the market some years ago, but had rejected the idea, thereby squandering a golden opportunity.

that a core competence would be developed internally. Apart from strengthening the awareness of the company's own core competences, these efforts helped to explore and define ideas or technologies to look for externally. In addition, marketing played an increasingly significant role in the innovation process, as it was responsible for understanding and appraising customer needs. Marketing had a gate-keeper function, whereas R&D's main responsibility was to convert identified customer needs into new products.

Customer-driven innovation

Long before the concept of *user-driven product development and design* was popularized, it had been a cornerstone of Coloplast's product development efforts. Ideas and knowledge from end-users, nurses, and surgeons served as critical inputs for new product development and fine-tuning. In fact, end-user understanding was a thread throughout the product development process and was continuously tested through organized discussion fora and efforts to gain insight into the end-users' day-to-day lives. Arguably, Coloplast's ability to incorporate the voices of end-users, nurses, and physicians was a distinctive competitive advantage and had resulted in numerous prizes for creative product designs: "Coloplast was founded on the understanding of user-needs and it is something deeply embedded in our culture. It means that the patient is involved in all stages in product development" (Lars Seier Christensen, Director of External Relations, *Børsen Magazine*, March 21, 2007). For example, in 2004, the company won the ID (Innovation through Design) prize for a catheter for women that was integrated into a package roughly the size and appearance of a lipstick tube. Another example was the design of compression underpants, which were targeted at ostomy patients with hernias.

The involvement of professionals and end-users in various boards and fora was an integrated part of Coloplast's innovation model, which consisted of front-end innovation, effective use of the AIM (Analyze, Improve, and Monitor) process (new product development) and global roll-outs following FIGARO (From Innovation to Accelerated Global Roll-Out) (see Figure 5.8). Products like SenSura, Conveen Optima, and Biatain Ibu were all results of this innovation model. The fora included Coloplast's Ostomy Forum (COF), which was undertaken in twenty countries and involved 400 stoma care nurses, the Wound Advisory Forum (WAF), which covered ten countries and

	Front-End Innovation	New Product Development	Global Roll-Out
Mission	• Adequate creativity, efforts, and resources based on strong customer inputs	• Accelerating the actual product development at the right time, quality, and price	• Global roll-out of new products—efficient, competitive, and customer-oriented
Process/ content	• Opportunity identification • Opportunity analysis • Idea generation & enrichment • Idea selection • Concept definition	Stage/gate model with five phases: 1. Idea formulation 2. Concept formulation 3. Product development 4. Test marketing 5. International marketing	• Communication platform • Global visuals • USPs • Positioning • Price strategy • Local adaptation and execution
Goals 2008	• Ten substantial new product ideas enter New Product Development	• Time to market of a new product: twenty-five months	• Within first year of a product launch to reach 70% of global market potential

Source: Information based on Coloplast presentation

FIGURE 5.8 Coloplast's innovation model

included 150 wound management nurses and doctors, and the Clinical Advisory Board (CAB), which had a presence in thirteen countries and 130 Continence Care nurses as participants.

In particular, the involvement of nurses in the COFs was extensive and systematic. For ten years, Coloplast had engaged nurses around the world in various boards via the COFs. The boards typically consisted of twelve to fourteen nurses. Project managers and development engineers from Coloplast met twice a year with each board in one- to two-day sessions with the purpose of brainstorming and eventually prioritizing ideas for improvements. Subsequently, Coloplast compared input from different geographical regions and synthesized the main ideas, which in turn served as final inputs for the product development department. This type of collaboration was iterative. Coloplast could, for instance, present prototypes based on input from previous years to obtain the nurses' critical opinions and ideas for further fine-tuning. The COFs were relatively resource-intensive and expensive to maintain and develop. Nevertheless, Coloplast believed that by engaging nurses in this way, new products would be optimized and product preferences would be established. Furthermore, the sessions helped instill some sense of ownership and commitment among the nurses.

While this approach to innovation indisputably yielded compelling results, many of the innovations fell victim to the fact that they were incremental by nature. In other words, they represented step-by-step improvements in safety, functionality, aesthetics, and discretion, but they were not groundbreaking. Customers referred to Coloplast as "the king of constant improvements" (customer interviews undertaken in connection with the recent organizational changes). At the COFs, nurses typically discussed patient *needs*, but they had difficulties in thinking outside the box. Similarly, interpreting an interview with an ostomy patient would probably bring about ideas on how to improve the adhesive or ease of removal, but it would not provide a novel approach to fundamentally rethinking the ostomy bag. This was, perhaps, Coloplast's challenge in a nutshell. The company's long-term and fruitful relationship with nurses, end-users, and other critical stakeholders was a powerful catalyst for incremental innovation. However, when it came to revolutionary innovations, the benefits were less evident. End-users, nurses, and physicians were simply not capable of articulating or conceptualizing fundamentally new approaches or ideas.

More recently, Coloplast engaged a group of anthropologists whose responsibilities were to observe and map the routines of ostomy patients and to come up with new product ideas. The anthropological method represented a fundamentally new approach to investigating end-users and was more reflective than previously tested methodologies. Expectations were high but it is still too early to evaluate experiences.

External R&D

In order to better be able to connect to external innovation environments, Coloplast established a specialized unit, External R&D, to handle all open innovation activities including technology scouting, external innovation partnerships, in-licensing, and out-licensing. The primary responsibilities of External R&D were to monitor external product development and to identify new technological opportunities and partners. The technology scouting unit evaluated the relevance of all external R&D enquiries for Coloplast's business areas. The overall objective of External R&D was not radical innovation *per se*, but access to the ideas, technologies, competences, and patents needed to solve a specific user need. A key criterion for success was that the open innovation activities complemented and strengthened internal knowledge, resources, and competences.

Open and external innovation activities were relatively new to Coloplast. As the head of Global R&D noted: "The R&D initiatives, as part of our organizational reshuffle, have had important implications for our business. We have moved towards a model where we – via Coloplast's organizational set-up – can accelerate the power and speed of external innovation environments/partners. At the same time, we seek to strengthen our ability to identify, understand and tap the external knowledge available" (interview with John Raabo

Nielsen, Senior Vice-President, Global R&D, February 11, 2008). Having established links to external innovation environments, the key challenge was to examine how new ideas and technologies could enrich internal R&D programs: "A key process step in 'digesting' external innovation involves translating these technologies and their implications for Coloplast into a language that employees can relate to. To be successful, we need to be crystal clear about the ways in which external innovation can be aligned with Coloplast's problem set and thus eventually enrich and inspire our own R&D efforts" (*ibid.*).

Incubation

The restructuring of the R&D resulted in the creation of an Incubation unit, which was part of the company's open innovation strategy. The unit served to cultivate new ideas and invest in less mature technologies outside of Coloplast's traditional markets. These ideas and technologies were to offer potential benefits for the company's business areas over a longer time period. According to CCO Lars Rasmussen, the aim was to tap into ideas at an early stage to modify and adapt them to Coloplast. Evidently, uncertainties existed as to whether the ideas and technologies would mature and reach the market, but to mitigate risks, Coloplast engaged in various partnerships. Via the Incubation unit, it exposed itself to potentially radical new ideas or products that could fundamentally alter the everyday lives of users.

Coloplast had identified three interesting areas: 1) Medical monitoring and diagnostics; 2) biomaterials and tissue engineering; and 3) medical delivery systems. In particular, Coloplast's investment in Interface Biotech, a company specialized in primary human tissue cell culturing, such as bone and cartilage, appeared promising. One of their R&D programs involved the extraction and cultivation of healthy cartilage tissues, which would then be inserted into knee joints to accelerate recovery from cartilage disorders. Apart from the financial investment, Coloplast provided the scaffold, i.e., the structure in the material on which the cultivated cartilage cells were mounted prior to insertion. In addition, Interface gained access to Coloplast's extensive knowledge base concerning regulations and patents. Coloplast hoped that this research, as well as the research with stem cells that was undertaken in cooperation with several Danish hospitals and universities, would increasingly prove applicable to the company's business areas, although there were no guarantees.

New Business Lab (NEBULA)

A number of years ago, Coloplast established the New Business Lab (NEBULA) to ignite a more radical approach to technological and market innovation. NEBULA was composed of four development engineers and four employees with a more commercial mindset. In general, the group was free from internal political bureaucracy and was quite diverse, with outsiders recruited to challenge conventional thinking. The assignment was unambiguous: To come up with ostomy care product ideas that would generate around DKK 2 billion in revenue by 2012. With substantial financial backing, the project group was not subject to limitations of any kind. However, this *laissez-faire* organizational setting caused some collaboration problems in the group, which had a negative impact on the output. Moreover, it proved difficult to obtain the necessary buy-in when sharing ideas with the traditional product development department, which often found the documentation and information to be inadequate. It was as if these tentative innovations or project ideas prompted more questions than answers and, consequently, they failed to adapt to the traditional Coloplast business model. NEBULA was eventually closed down, having set in motion three projects and generating revenue of DKK 20 million.

With previous attempts to promote a more open approach to innovation in mind, CEO Sten Scheibye thought that employees' mental maps needed to embrace an unconventional line of thinking. Would the increasing focus on applying lean principles throughout the organization harm creativity? Management could not communicate a burning platform – overall, business was good. How could Coloplast encourage unorthodoxy and creativity in times characterized by high contribution ratios? The plethora of initiatives that Coloplast launched, including a major organizational restructuring, the setup of external R&D and incubator units, and the involvement of anthropologists, would not only strengthen the company's internal innovative capabilities but would also embrace R&D environments outside the company's field of operation. However, Coloplast also needed to balance its competences within incremental innovation with its aspirations to break new ground. For instance, would it, with its long-standing relationship with nurses who constituted a powerful source of inspiration, be able to further develop this forum and inspire a higher degree of creative thinking? Or would "the ties that bind may become the ties that blind?"[4]

COLOPLAST: SUMMARY AND QUESTIONS FOR DISCUSSION

Coloplast is a global producer of medical equipment operating in three business areas related to intimate healthcare. The company operates in markets where the demographic developments are favorable considering their product portfolio. Traditionally, Coloplast's strategy has focused on cost reductions and efficiency in the organization, just as efficiency has been improved by the implementation of lean manufacturing principles throughout the organization. In recent years it has invested in production facilities in Hungary and China in order to transfer production from Denmark to these low-cost areas. In addition, it made a significant acquisition in the USA, strengthening its global position. In all, the company has moved 85 percent of its production outside Denmark (i.e., to Hungary, China, and the USA) in order to maintain a competitive business. Furthermore, the company has increased its investments in research and development in order to reach its goal of being a first mover.

In 2007, Coloplast launched its biggest organizational restructuring in twenty-three years, which affected most of the company's

---

[4] Adopted from D. Cohen and L. Prusak, *In Good Company: How Social Capital Makes Organizations Work* (Cambridge, MA: Harvard Business School Press, 2001).

employees, product divisions, and business areas. Coloplast was originally a Danish company with operations mainly in Europe, but with its recent expansions it was becoming a truly global company with value chain functions scattered all over the world and a growing position as a global market leader. While the relocation of production was well underway, other areas, such as R&D, sales, and marketing were on the threshold of becoming more standardized and global. The big question was how the company could become more standardized on a global scale without compromising creativity in R&D, sales, and marketing. Internal innovation and dialog has always been a big part of Coloplast's way of doing business. This has over time resulted in a number of improvements to existing products and hence has caused the company to be labeled as the "king of constant improvements." Coloplast was in dialog with nurses, doctors, wholesalers, retailers, and the end-users themselves on product improvements. But it was rarely the case that truly new innovations emerged from this collaboration, which encouraged the company to search for a broader external environment supporting new innovations. So, as part of the new strategy, Coloplast wanted to expand the foundation for innovation by forging new relations between the external environments and the internal R&D. The challenge was both to avoid the development of a "not invented here" syndrome and leverage the advantages that follow from growing globalization. As such, the case facilitates discussion of the following issues:

1. Coloplast wanted to adopt a more standardized global approach considering sales, marketing, and R&D.
   a. In which way could standardization compromise the internal creativity?
   b. What were the pros and cons that could be found in the organizational shift from matrix to functional lines?
2. Internal innovation and dialog had always been a big part of Coloplast's way of doing business. This has over time resulted in a number of improvements to existing products and thus caused the company to be labeled as the "king of constant improvements."
   a. What measures were taken to avoid the "not invented here" syndrome and to be more open to external product ideas?

b. What was the role of middle management during the expansion of R&D to include external sources of innovation and connect to internal R&D?

c. What has become a key competitive advantage for Coloplast? How can such a competitive advantage backfire?

3. Coloplast saw a huge potential in entering the US market and it started to expand through strategic acquisitions.

a. How did Coloplast rethink its acquisitions as an integrated strategy?

b. What were the advantages of entering the US market?

c. What did the takeover of Mentor mean to Coloplast?

d. Can acquisitions be used as a future strategy for Coloplast? What is meant by "it is not like a supermarket?"

4. The commercial excellence group was one of many functions to help Coloplast to become more standardized and it worked as a support function professionalizing Coloplast's approach to selling.

a. What was the function of the commercial excellence group?

b. What difficulties occurred with the launch of the commercial excellence function?

c. What did top management do to overcome the potential resistance against the function?

5. Looking at the future development for Coloplast on a global scale, which areas of management innovation could be envisioned for Coloplast in the future?

a. When business is performing well, how can employees be encouraged toward unorthodoxy and creativity to ensure future growth?

b. What are the most critical barriers for continuous high growth in the future?

ADDITIONAL SOURCES IN RELATION TO COLOPLAST

www.coloplast.com

Andersen, P. H. (2005) "Relationship marketing and brand involvement of professionals through web-enhanced brand communities: The case of Coloplast," *Industrial Marketing Management*, 34(1), 39–51.

Kragh, P. (2008). *How to Involve Users in Front End of Innovation: Methods to Get Success in Innovation Work*. Coloplast.

Pyndt, J. and Pedersen, T. (2005). *Managing Global Offshoring Strategies: A Case Approach*. Copenhagen Business School Press.

6   Chr. Hansen: Collaborative forms under private equity ownership

> "I am completely convinced that the private equity model, if executed correctly, results in better ownership, more efficiently run businesses and increased returns for investors. Committed and active ownership is all about having a very close relationship with management and the appointment of external Board members that act as [a] qualified sounding board, both to management of the portfolio company and to the private equity fund, in order to create clear and achievable strategic and operational plan[s] for the business."
>
> Lars Terney, partner, Nordic Capital in Denmark (*Børsen*, January 28, 2008)

To be frank, the CEO of Chr. Hansen, Lars Frederiksen, could not understand the general public's harsh and emotional critique of private equity funds (PEF). Accusations were plentiful: World champions in asset stripping loading their investment objects with exorbitant amounts of debt only to suck out capital for investors! Aggressive cost-cutters ignoring employees and suppliers! Moreover, PEFs were infamous for their aggressive tax planning. Indeed, they were routinely charged with all sorts of iniquities. However, the main reason for the unfavorable light in which PEFs were portrayed in the media was related to the fact that they were a relatively new phenomenon in the Danish business community. Perhaps the fear of the unknown meant that public and media attention tended to be one-sided.

According to Frederiksen, the reality of PEFs was more complex. Each PEF was distinct and pursued different strategies, making it unfair to make naïve generalizations. He felt that the story of Chr. Hansen offered an interesting glimpse into the workings of PEFs. The 2005 delisting of Chr. Hansen's ingredients activities from the Copenhagen Stock Exchange following the DKK 8.2 billion takeover by the French PEF, PAI Partners, marked the beginning of a self-examination process that was remarkably "healthy" and helped to reshape the company.

Following the takeover, Frederiksen was appointed CEO. With the assistance of external consultants and in close collaboration with PAI Partners, he took an active role in assessing both managerial capabilities and the organizational idiosyncrasies that were inhibiting development. The process was invigorating and delivered solid results. In 2006/7, sales amounted to DKK 3.709 million and EBIDTA was DKK 906 million (a 24 percent increase on the previous year). This was the second consecutive year of significant top-line and EBITDA growth. Meeting PAI's financial expectations was satisfactory in itself, but Frederiksen was particularly thrilled by the way in which the results had been achieved. His monthly business reviews in Copenhagen or Paris and his weekly dialogs with PAI were highly constructive, as the PAI professionals were extremely familiar with Chr. Hansen's business operations. They were therefore able to discuss critical business issues, enabling the executive management to make better and more informed decisions. The cooperation was fruitful. The shift to private ownership had allowed Frederiksen to allocate most of his managerial effort to the main businesses, free from the pressures of the stock market, the media, and equity analysts. He did not have to placate the market from quarter to quarter, a fact that allowed for write-offs, divestments, or large investments that were not necessarily accretive in the first two years.

However, the situation was not entirely rosy for Chr. Hansen. While the change to private equity ownership had provided strong incentives on the management level, Frederiksen was concerned with two issues:

1. The ownership change had unleashed a great deal of organizational energy, but it had also invoked a "tougher" culture with a greater focus on performance and value creation. These changes had quite an impact on the employees. Some left the company while others struggled to accommodate the new organizational environment. The question facing Frederiksen was how to encourage all employees to buy into the project of reshaping Chr. Hansen under private equity ownership. Every employee

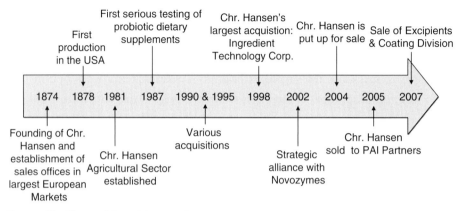

Source: Chr. Hansen internal documents

FIGURE 6.1 Historical timeline

knew that PAI's involvement would be provisional. How could he, as CEO, craft and sell the message, while also creating adequate incentives and a strong work ethic?

2. On an organizational level, Frederiksen's main concern related to the extent to which the momentum could be maintained when PAI executed its exit strategy. The common perception was that PAI had ignited dynamism and energy. Would this dynamism flounder when ownership changed and, if so, how could the company prepare for that in the best possible way?

CHR. HANSEN'S HISTORY

Chr. Hansen was founded in 1874 in Copenhagen by the Danish pharmacist Christian D.A. Hansen. His research led to the development of a process to extract a pure and standardized rennet enzyme from calves' stomachs, which was eventually used to make cheese. He established his first rennet factory in 1874 and soon began to produce natural colors for butter and cheese (www.chr-hansen.com) (see Figure 6.1).

Chr. Hansen was international from the outset. Companies or agents in France, Italy, and the UK were established soon after the company was founded, and the first processing plant was set up in 1878 in the US state of New York. As of 2007, the company employed 2,500 people in over thirty countries, with distributors and agents located worldwide. The major basic research facilities are located in Denmark, while production sites are scattered around the globe in such countries as Brazil, Denmark, France, Italy, Germany, Peru, and the USA.

Omnipresent yet unknown

Chr. Hansen is a global market leader in the production of enzymes for cheese production (rennet) and cultures for the dairy, wine, and meat industries. The company also holds approximately 30 percent of the global market for natural colors. Its natural ingredient solutions are utilized in the food, pharmaceutical, nutritional, and agricultural industries. More than 500 million people around the world actually consume Chr. Hansen's products every day, but it is virtually unknown to ordinary people. The company's products are used in one-third of all cheeses made worldwide, while more than half of all yogurt consumed globally includes its cultures. The very popular probiotic cultures section offers the company strong growth opportunities. In addition, Chr. Hansen provides a range of colors for the ice cream and dessert industry, seeking to incorporate consumer trends and market developments. Within the meat industry, it supplies cultures, colors, and functional blends, all of which seek to improve the flavor, appearance, texture, and stability of the finished meat products.

The company is organized around four product divisions: Cultures & Enzymes, Natural Colors, Flavors, and Health & Nutrition (see Figure 6.2 and Table 6.1). The Health and Nutrition division was established in 2007 in order to move the company's technology platform into new health applications. Targeting the global market for dietary supplements, its task is to develop probiotic products that *improve the quality of food and health for people all over the world*, in accordance with the company's vision.

Prior to the divestment of the ingredients business, Chr. Hansen's holding company also owned ALK-Abelló – a specialized world leader within the field of allergy vaccinations (allergen

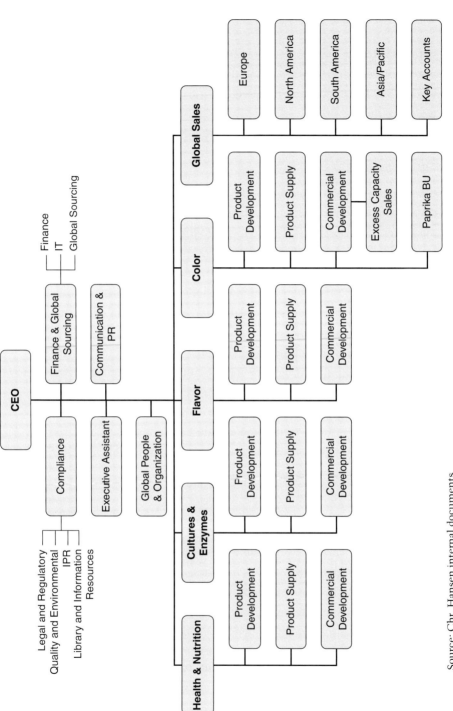

Source: Chr. Hansen internal documents

FIGURE 6.2 Organizational structure

Table 6.1 *Chr. Hansen's position in various business segments (2005)*

	Top players	Market size (DKK million)	Relative market share (% of world market)[*]	Market growth
Cultures	1. Chr. Hansen	4,050	1.6	7–8%
	2. Danisco			
	3. Degussa			
Dairy enzymes (coagulants)	1. Chr. Hansen	1,000	1.3[**]	–3%
	2. DSM			
	3. Danisco			
Natural colors	1. Chr. Hansen	2,120	1.2	4%
	2. Sensient			
Flavors	1. Givaudan	46,000	0.1	3–4%
	2. IFF			
	3. Symrise			

[*] Chr. Hansen market share compared to market leader or next biggest player, if Chr. Hansen is market leader.
[**] Relative market share in volume (Medical Intermediate Care Unit [MIMCU]) is estimated to be 1.13.
Source: Chr. Hansen internal documents

immunotherapy). In 2004–5, ALK-Abelló put significant efforts into developing safer, more convenient tablet-based vaccines founded on a more pharmaceutical approach. The new business area had significant potential, yet it was capital-intensive, absorbing approximately DKK 200 million in R&D.

Sluggish performance: Preparing for sale

When the board first addressed the issue of splitting the company into two focused entities – Chr. Hansen and ALK-Abelló – in 2004, it was by no means clear that Chr. Hansen would be sold to a PEF.

Preliminary discussions evolved around the possibility of listing the allergy division as an independent entity. Market analysts had long envisaged a promising future for ALK-Abelló, expecting that a listing would create a "world-leading allergy vaccine company with [a] highly profitable business and pipeline offering a paradigm shift in allergy vaccination treatment" (*Danske Equities*, May 26, 2004). At the same time, expectations for the ingredient business were not so glamorous.

During the 1990s, Chr. Hansen had embarked on an aggressive expansion via acquisitions and capacity increases, which had drained managerial resources and squeezed profit margins. This strategy resulted in the expansion of the product portfolio into new areas such as sweeteners and pharmaceutical excipients, areas in which the company had no previous experience. In response to the mediocre financial performance of the company, selected production facilities were closed, product categories were trimmed, and the customer base was slimmed down – all initiatives that helped to improve the financial situation. However, the company's EBITA margins were still approximate three percentage points behind its industry peers (see Table 6.2). From 2002 to 2004, its net sales dropped –2.42 percent CAGR,[1] while EBITA showed a minor improvement of 1.87 percent CAGR. This development mirrored the deliberate focus on profitability at the expense of growth. In particular, North American sales declined although European revenue saw a slight pick-up during this period (see Figures 6.3 and 6.4 for a detailed view of the financial situation prior to the sell-off).

His twenty-five years of experience with the company left CEO Lars Frederiksen with a vivid impression of the situation at that point. In his mind, Chr. Hansen had become a "sleepy" and "dusty" company in which employees were somewhat complacent. It was slow to adapt to new technologies and lacked a focused strategy. Despite its aspirations to become an international player, the alignment between headquarters

---

[1] Compound Annual Growth Rate (CAGR) denotes the year-on-year growth rate applied to an investment or other part of a company's activities over a multiple-year period.

Table 6.2 *Margins for food ingredients manufacturers in 2004*

	EBITDA margin	EBITA margin	EBIT margin
Danisco Ingredients	21.0%	15.4%	12.2%
Chr. Hansen	17.7%	12.6%	10.6%
Novozymes	26.2%	17.3%	16.8%
IFF	19.4%	15.4%	14.7%
Sensient	20.0%	15.8%	15.6%
Quest (ICI)	n.a.	11.5%	n.a.
DSM	17.6%	n.a.	10.7%
Givaudan	21.7%	18.4%	15.1%
Degussa	15.0%	n.a.	8.6%
Average	*19.8%*	*15.2%*	*13%*

Note: Numbers for DSM include products other than food ingredients.

Source: Company accounts and *Danske Equities,* May, 2004

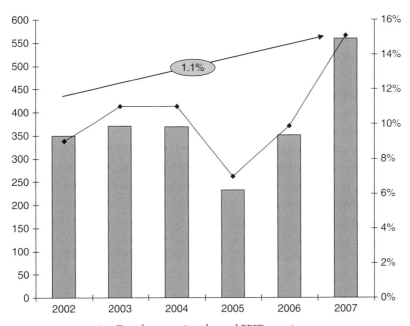

a) EBIT Development (MDKK)

FIGURE 6.3 Development in sales and EBIT margins

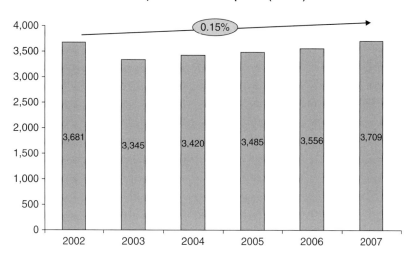

b) Net sales development (MDKK)

x% = CAGR
Note: Financial year ends September 30
Net sales development CAGR 2002–4 = –2.42%
EBIT development CAGR 2002–4 = 1.87%

Source: Chr. Hansen annual reports

FIGURE 6.3 (cont.)

and the local subsidiaries was poor, with the latter often acting as local kingdoms. Moreover, an apparent silo mentality dominated the organization. Nevertheless, most employees were proud to be part of the company. They would point to Chr. Hansen's unique culture, which was characterized by a high degree of cohesion and a "feel-good" working climate. However, it was also a culture that left much to be desired in terms of human performance development. There were no "whip and carrot" principles built into the system – metrics and KPIs were hardly defined. In practice, this meant that poor employee performance had no consequences, which in turn created a lack of accountability in the organization. Poorly performing employees would typically be moved to another department and were only rarely fired. The high performers

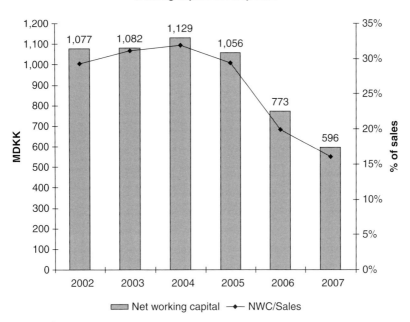

Working capital development

Source: Chr. Hansen annual reports

FIGURE 6.4 Development in working capital 2002–7

found this highly provocative and their motivation was hamstrung. Therefore, the platform was burning from both financial and cultural viewpoints. As Frederiksen remarked: "The sense of urgency or the near-death experience at Chr. Hansen was evident. Something drastic was needed to stir the waters and give the company a wake-up call" (interview with CEO Lars Frederiksen, January 14, 2008).

Speculations of a sell-off accelerated within the Board when the majority shareholder, the Lundbeck Foundation (holding a 35.2 percent stake and 64.2 percent of the votes), announced in November 2004 that it did not see itself as a long-term strategic shareholder in an ingredients company. The sales process could begin.

Initially, competitors and industrial players were mentioned as potential acquirers. For instance, the Ireland-based Kerry Group, the

Dutch DSM, or Danisco were expected to show interest. Market analysts estimated an initial selling price of DKK 5.3–7.2 billion, but they were soon to re-evaluate their estimates. When the process came to a close in late April 2005, the group of interested buyers had extended to include such investment funds as EQT, Blackstone, and Apax Partners. It was the French-based PEF, PAI Partners – one of the oldest PEFs in Europe, specializing in consumer goods and services sectors – that carried off the ingredients business by offering DKK 8.2 billion. The main shareholders and the Board were more than satisfied. Led by a Senior Partner, Bertrand Meunier, PAI's intention was to maintain the decision centre in Hørsholm, Denmark and "to grow the business through continued expansion of the geographic market coverage, investment in capacity and R&D as well as potential add-on acquisitions" (press release, April 29, 2005). Elaborating retrospectively, former Chr. Hansen Chairman Jørgen Worning noted that "we saw the consolidation in the ingredients market and decided to join in the consolidation. We felt we should concentrate on pharmaceuticals. We ran a very good sale process and achieved a very good multiple of 13 times EBITDA" (www.thedeal.com, May 2, 2005).

PAI TAKES OVER CHR. HANSEN

Following a due diligence process in which PAI's team of advisers systematically scrutinized the company, a number of analytical and strategic exercises were set in motion. The process forced Chr. Hansen's management into self-examination and the unraveling of organizational idiosyncrasies. According to Lars Frederiksen, the process was rewarding yet demanding, as no business procedures or management routines were held sacred. Management was constantly challenged: "When you are asked the same annoying question eight times or so, you start [to] consider whether it is the question or the answer that is rubbish" (Lars Frederiksen, *Børsen*, October 7, 2005).

First, Chr. Hansen engaged the renowned management recruiting and assessment company Egon Zehnder International to compile over fifty management appraisals as well as a review of the company's culture and values. The conclusions revealed that Chr. Hansen had historically been under-managed and that a strong human performance culture and accountability were absent. At the same time, the results showed great human capital potential and a strong willingness to do things differently within the management group.

Second, the company teamed up with Boston Consulting Group (BCG) to conduct an organizational review in order to fine-tune and validate the strategy, and to provide recommendations for the organizational setup. BCG had advised one of the potential acquirers in the bidding process and it had demonstrated a strong understanding of Chr. Hansen and the challenges that characterized the food ingredients industry. In terms of strategic direction, management and PAI had to evaluate the company's core competences in order to identify where Chr. Hansen had competitive advantages vis-à-vis its competitors. While management felt strongly about the culture and enzymes business in terms of strategic fit, platform, and market positioning, the business areas of flavors, colors, and animal and human health called for more radical changes. These findings relied on a good dose of self-awareness, as indicated by Frederiksen: "We manage business models well in which there is a high degree of value added in the products, high margins and relatively small volumes. Our US sweetener activities do not fit this scheme as they are characterized by low margins and large volumes. There is nothing wrong with this niche. We just do not know how to run it profitably" (*Børsen*, October 5, 2005). BCG's work resulted in a number of strategic priorities, including to "expand leadership" within cultures, to turn around and grow colors via profitability optimization and market expansion, and to reshape the flavor business by focusing on existing markets and customers. In addition, business areas in which Chr. Hansen could not add value were to be divested. These priorities were digested into five "must-win" battles if Chr. Hansen was to honor the objectives (see Figure 6.5).

With respect to organizational structure, BCG's advice led to a product-oriented organization. In terms of margins, industry focus,

High, but focused growth	• 8% organic growth per year • Acquisitions in core business • Divest non-core activities
Create value in all businesses	• Turnaround in Colors and Flavors • Improve cash generation and reduce net working capital • Technology and innovation leadership
Strong value chain integration and close customer contact	• Implement new organization effectively • Local sales with customer focus through industry segments • Stronger Industry Technology Centers
Be lean – execute – measure	• Streamline all steps of value chain • Stop unproductive activities • Set "SMART" goals, measure, and follow-up
Proactively drive people development	• Systematic career and talent management • Low performance not permitted; superior performance rewarded • Keep nurturing our "can do and want to win attitude"

SMART = Specific, Measurable, Actionable, Relevant, and
   Time-limited
Source: Chr. Hansen internal documents

FIGURE 6.5 Chr. Hansen's "must-win" battles laid down in immediate continuation of the takeover

market position and approach, and industry dynamics, Chr. Hansen's product areas varied widely. For example, while the market for cultures was driven by intellectual property-protected fermentation technology and was characterized by high gross margins (50–60 percent), stable raw material prices, and high entry barriers, the business model for colors involved lower gross margins (20–40 percent), fluctuating raw material prices, low entry barriers, and, in general, the products were regarded as commodities. Thus, each product area had a fundamentally different logic, which was difficult to harness through a functional setup.

A global division was established within the sales department as an attempt to standardize and professionalize as well as to draw in competent employees. In addition, globalizing sales was meant to counteract the engineering mindset permeating Chr. Hansen. The explicit product focus allowed for increased target traceability and transparency in performance. The product orientation meant that the company deliberately deselected the "one-stop supplier" strategy that was actively pursued by competitors. According to Frederiksen, value creation was achieved through product excellence rather than through a "one size fits all" strategy.

In sum, the consulting efforts helped to shape the "new" Chr. Hansen, to set strategic direction to assess managerial capabilities, and to identify development areas. The process was vital to harnessing the "stickiness" of Chr. Hansen's organizational heritage, which would bode well for a new beginning.

Cooperative ties between PAI and Chr. Hansen

PAI's acquisition of Chr. Hansen marked the beginning of a constructive working relationship and demonstrated how ties may function between a PEF and the acquired company. According to Lars Frederiksen, this involved an intensified focus on value creation and accountability, delegation, selection of the right team, provision of strong incentives, and the focus of managerial efforts on key business challenges.

Creating value through strategic sparring

In simplified terms, PEFs may cash in on their investments following one of two quite distinct strategies. On the one hand, they can embark on heavy borrowing and slice costs, a strategy referred to as "milking the cow," but this is a risky strategy as assets may shrink. PAI investments typically follow another strategy, as seen with Chr. Hansen. Bertrand Meunier, a Senior Partner at PAI, described the strategy as one in which investments were made in global market leaders. Subsequent efforts were aimed at "increasing the strategic value of the company through top-line growth superior to any other player in the market" (*Berlingske Tidende*, October 25, 2007). These intentions were well understood within Chr. Hansen's management group. PAI's ownership and involvement could be compared to investing in a property that would be sold off some years later because "then you do your utmost to maintain it properly and eventually invest in a new kitchen so the house does not lose value" (*ibid.*). At the beginning of 2007, when the business media speculated in asset stripping, the real estate analogy came in handy: "We refinanced ourselves. Just as you would if your house was financed by a mortgage loan and an expensive bank loan. In our case, the value of the company increased, so we refinanced to get rid of the expensive share-holder debt. Not a single krone has been drained" (*ibid.*). Chr. Hansen's 2006 refinancing operation meant that the net interest-bearing debt increased by DKK 1.865 million to a total of DKK 6.590 million.

PAI's acquisition team took an active role in further developing Chr. Hansen. Monthly business reviews, with the participation of CEO Lars Frederiksen and CFO Henning Jakobsen, were organized in Paris or Copenhagen. Typical issues up for discussion in these meetings included status, strategic priorities, and critical action areas. Depending on the type of issues involved, the CEO and CFO usually teamed up with one or two other members of the executive group, but a business development manager could also be seen, infusing the business review process with more operational knowledge of how a strategic project was progressing in a specific area. The fact that PAI's people were highly skilled and knowl-edgeable about the industry made these sessions extremely rewarding. They were able to challenge planned decisions, projects, and analyses in a constructive way. In addition to formalized business reviews, Frederiksen had conversations with PAI Partner Frédéric Stévenin several times a week, during which urgent issues, ideas, and thoughts were evaluated. As the head of PAI's Consumer Goods Group and given his long experience in working with private equity companies focusing on the food industry, he served as a sparring partner for Frederiksen, who found inspiration in these dialogs. PAI's close super-vision and involvement did not bring about more bureaucracy (i.e., in terms of approvals). In its role as owner, PAI monitored business deci-sions closely, but general management at Chr. Hansen was given rela-tively free rein.

The Board comprised four PAI representatives, Lars Frederiksen, and three employee representatives. It aimed to help management shape and execute strategy. It was also far more involved in assisting the company when compared to traditional public boards, which are mainly concerned with fulfilling governance requirements and overseeing the management of the business in order to enhance share-holder value. The palpable overlap in Board representatives and partic-ipants in monthly business reviews and weekly sparring sessions accelerated the decision-making process and assured symmetrical information. When the company needed a new chairman in 2006, Frederiksen preferred a PAI representative rather than an external candidate. He wished to avoid the possibility that asymmetrical infor-mation would slow down business operations. Eventually, PAI Partner and Head of Consumer Goods, Frédéric Stévenin, assumed the role as Chairman of the Board (see Figure 6.6).

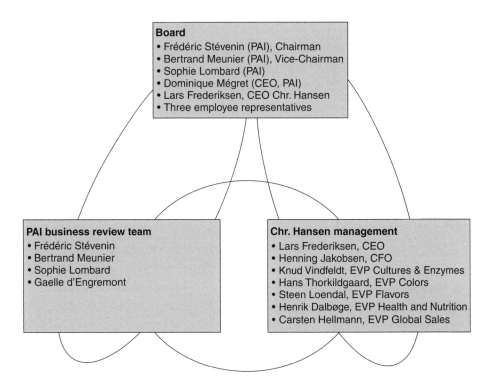

Source: Own drawing based on interview with Lars Frederiksen, January 14, 2008

FIGURE 6.6 Collaborative ties between PAI, the Board, and management

In sum, the close collaborative ties between management, PAI, and the Board enabled Chr. Hansen to respond to changes quickly. Being generally free from the pressures of the stock market, analysts, and the media, the company could execute critical business decisions, such as closing a plant or divesting a business activity, without having to consider the reactions on the stock exchange. Furthermore, it could react swiftly if unexpected incidents called for action.

Delegation within fixed boundaries

One notable difference following PAI's involvement related to the degree of delegation within a well-defined organizational setup. Previously, local subsidiaries had enjoyed a high degree of autonomy with little interference from headquarters. The balance of autonomy changed following PAI's takeover. Given the scope of change, strong, clear guidelines were needed to get all organizational units and employees working in the same direction toward common goals. This meant that management needed to be crystal clear and conscious about which type of setup would engender the desired change to take place locally. The strategy, guidelines, and interfaces were defined at the top. However, when operating within this setup, local management teams were relatively free to carry out their own ideas and projects. When PAI put Frederiksen at the helm of Chr. Hansen, it wanted a firm, team-oriented leader who could set the direction and establish common ground throughout the organization. Frederiksen himself was aware of the dual role: "The new owners make high demands. I am a team-oriented leader. I do not order my employees about in any way I choose. I want to coach them and I assign them high-level responsibilities, which in turn brings about good results" (*Børsen*, May 4, 2005).

Management reshuffle

With respect to the management team at Chr. Hansen, it was not "business as usual." Lars Frederiksen came into the CEO position having previously held the role of Executive Vice-President (Business

Operations). CFO Leif Nørgaard, HR Director Eigil Conradsen, and the former Head of International Operations, Group Vice-President Jan Boeg Hansen, all left the company for various reasons. The replacement of these executives was handled through a combination of internal recruitments and external hirings. In particular, the recruitment of Henning Jakobsen as CFO (who had fifteen years of experience at Colgate) and a new head of People & Organization (HR), Jesper Allentoft, in 2005 was remarkable. The latter marked a shift in the way in which HR was perceived at Chr. Hansen. According to Frederiksen, previously the company had "a sort of hiring-firing organization with some attempts at organizational development but without a clear strategy." The new HR executive needed to establish a revised vision, to place HR on the senior management agenda, and to align various processes, including recruiting, performance appraisals, and compensation, on a global scale. Therefore, the recruitment of Allentoft underlined an explicit focus on performance and employee development, and signified a serious attempt to professionalize HR within Chr. Hansen.[2]

While the business media found the management reshuffle fairly dramatic, Frederiksen remarked that the novel composition of the management group was an invigorating source of inspiration that had brought with it new perspectives and discussions. The new management setup was roughly composed of one-third "newcomers" or "outsiders," one-third "oldies" and one-third "talented lions from within the organization," as the CEO put it (interview with Lars Frederiksen, January 14, 2008). PAI was deeply involved in the process of establishing the right team and supported the idea of backing inherent management capacity while also installing a few outside managers.

---

[2] Readers interested in a detailed description of the HR aspects of Chr. Hansen may consult Dana Minbaeva (Assistant Professor at Copenhagen Business School), "Chr. Hansen (A): From Danish Personnel Department of 1965 to Global State-of-the-Art HR Organization 2007" (unpublished case).

Strong incentives

While publicly owned companies often discuss appropriate indicators to measure performance, PEFs focus solely on top-line growth, cash, and margin improvements, a fact that helps to tighten management's focus. Following PAI's takeover of Chr. Hansen, clarity became the running theme. The roles and goals of the Board and owners were exceedingly well-defined and transparent, which in turn created a stronger awareness among the executive team of what should be accomplished. The goal was to achieve revenue of DKK 5 billion and an EBITDA margin of 30 percent by 2010, while keeping a constant focus reducing working capital and cash flows to optimize the balance.

The game was also serious in the sense that executive management members were required to invest a substantial chunk of their own funds into the deal. Unlike publicly listed companies, where typically executive pay is linked to performance via stock options with no downside, management in private equity companies is usually obliged to put in personal money at the same price as the PEF – with the same risk of losing money if things go wrong. This creates a feeling of ownership as opposed to a corporate mentality. Management is much more concerned with how invested money will grow business and, in some ways, is more willing to stretch itself to meet the outlined targets. For instance, at PAI's request, Frederiksen invested DKK 4 million of his own money. In his words, this involved higher stakes: "It provides me with an opportunity to gain a large profit, but there is also a substantial risk attached to it. In the worst case, I can lose all my invested money. Yet, I sincerely believe in the project and I am not afraid of losing it … now I go up and down with the company. It is not like an option program where you do not necessarily have to redeem them. Having DKK 4 million of your own money invested is another feeling" (*Berlingske Tidende*, September 6, 2005).

Communication free of bureaucracy

One notable change was related to internal communication which, according to Lars Frederiksen, had become more open and honest. It was as if the strong focus on commercial operations had made Chr. Hansen less political and bureaucratic. Frederiksen took advantage of this in his communication to employees. A monthly email, authored by him, providing a status update and highlighting strategic focus areas, was distributed to all staff. In addition, the email addressed a specific theme, such as Performance Development Interviews (PDIs), a concept implemented to enhance the focus on individual development plans and relate them to strategic business goals. Apart from regular meetings, Frederiksen also addressed financial performance in a monthly email specifically targeted at the top 100 managers. This mail discussed sales, earnings, net working capital, short-term challenges, and focus areas, and was sparked by the monthly business reviews with PAI. All this could be done without considering the communication and insider constraints facing a public company, where the stock market is the first to know. Frederiksen really enjoyed this communicative latitude, which he felt was more constructive and gave him valuable input: "We are free from using a lot of resources to tell the outside world about every single movement we make. My predecessor used approximately 25–30 percent of his time talking to analysts, which is a lot of time that could have been used to run the business" (*Børsen*, November 17, 2006).

Frederiksen also participated in the "High Performance Workshop" and "Leadership Development Program" internal management programs, which included 300 managers around the world, where he provided his view on thought leadership at Chr. Hansen. Local managers were often astounded when he showed up, but he regarded it as a unique opportunity to tap into local management routines and convey some of his personal leadership experiences at Chr. Hansen. The only caveat from a communication standpoint was that the business media had lost interest in the company following the takeover. It was almost impossible to persuade journalists to write about new product introductions. Journalists wanted sensational stories, which in Chr. Hansen's case were hard to access as the company was not obliged to publish information on significant events impacting financial performance.

EMPLOYEES: THE KEY TO EXECUTION

If Lars Frederiksen had one regret, it was his "business as usual" state-ment given immediately after PAI's takeover. Business was anything but usual! Moving to private ownership signaled drastic changes on many fronts, including strategy, the organizational setup, expectations for employee performance, and monitoring via KPIs – all initiatives to make employees accountable for their actions. Employee turnover was notable in 2005 and 2006. Some felt that the disintegration of the "good old" Chr. Hansen culture was unavoidable, while others did not approve of the explicit focus on financial performance. Still, many stayed, seeking to adapt. A takeover always stirs up emotions, but the obscurity of the content and timing of the next strategic move left many employees with mixed feelings. However, the employee survey performed in 2007 – two years after the takeover – showed a significant improvement in employee satisfaction and in the quality of middle managers as assessed by employees.

Although value creation prior to PAI's exit was a top priority for management, the message was somewhat downplayed in the commu-nication with employees. The risk was that some employees would feel they were working exceedingly hard only to create a "Potemkin village" that would falter soon after PAI's exit. Therefore, Frederiksen often stressed the issue of sustainability when communicating with employees. The developmental efforts of Chr. Hansen were aimed at building a strong company, one that would retain its strength even after PAI's exit. The introduction of PDIs served as a key instrument in building a stronger company, strengthening employees' competences while maintaining constant focus on performance. PDIs were held each year for employees and managers with the purpose of better connecting personal goals with the unit's goals and the overall strategy of the company. PDIs typically consisted of four steps: A follow-up on last year's targets, performance evaluation and salary adjustment, a definition of business targets for the next period, and preparation of an individual development plan (see Box 6.1).

BOX 6.1 **Introduction to PDIs**

Purpose of the interview

The purpose of the PDI is to ensure that every employee knows and understands the connection between their own tasks, the goals in the unit, and the overall strategy of Chr. Hansen. The interview ensures that the qualifications and competences of each employee are used and developed in the best possible way to the benefit of Chr. Hansen as well as the employee.

At Chr. Hansen we attach great importance to the development of our employees as they are key to our continued success. All employees must have a PDI and as an outcome an Individual Development Plan. To ensure consistency worldwide, the global PDI form should be used by all employees and managers in Chr. Hansen. The basis for the interview is a follow-up on the past year, i.e., agreed goals and tasks and development activities, if any. The interviews consist of four steps.

1. Follow-up on last year's targets and performance evaluation

The basis of the PDI is an evaluation of the employee's performance based on the targets agreed for last year. Subsequently, the employee's performance is evaluated in relation to the performance criteria for Chr. Hansen. It is important to thoroughly discuss what performance criteria can advantageously be enhanced to improve the performance for the next period. The interview should also touch on the subject of how the manager can best support the employee as regards development and how the employee experiences the cooperation with the manager.

2. Salary evaluation

The evaluation of last year's targets and the total performance evaluation of the employee form the basis of the determination of the salary for the next period. The salary will be communicated at the interview.

BOX 6.1 (CONTINUED)

3. Determination of business targets for the next period

On the basis of the targets set for the area/department, the employee and the manager agree on business targets for the next period. Each manager is responsible for ensuring that all employees in the area/department are informed about the overall targets for Chr. Hansen and understand how they contribute to the targets of the department.

The business targets must be well-defined and realistic, and can advantageously be set in accordance with the SMART model: **S** = Significant, **M** = Measurable, **A** = Ambitious, **R** = Realistic, and **T** = Time-limited.

Before the interview, the parties must consider which tasks to prioritize in the short term as well as in the long term. Furthermore, it can be considered if the employee is prepared and able to take on new tasks. Additionally, it should be discussed what support from the manager is required in order for the employee to fulfill the business targets.

4. Individual Development Plan

On the basis of the defined targets and the performance evaluation, the employee and the manager agree on future competence development initiatives, both in the short term and the long term. A number of elements go into preparing the individual development plan:

- The business targets and expectations for the next period.
- Future job requirements.
- Performance evaluation.
- Professional and personal competence development needs.
- Possible future job opportunities.

After the PDI, the employee enters the agreed targets and the Individual Development Plan for the next period, and both parties sign the forms. The manager and the employee are mutually responsible for implementation of the agreed targets.

Source: Chr. Hansen internal documents

Financial boost and recent developments

Judging by the financial achievements, the process was encouraging. From 2006 to 2007, revenue rose by 4 percent, organic growth was 10.2 percent, the EBITDA margin increased by 20.4 percent to 24.4 percent, and there was a positive net cash flow of DKK 24 million, despite investments totaling DKK 450 million. Working capital was reduced from 28 percent to 16 percent of sales. The sweetener, paprika, and excipients activities were divested. All regions and product groups experienced strong sales growth (see Table 6.3). As Lars Frederiksen noted: "Since the change in ownership two years ago, we have been working determinedly to focus the business and create growth, and I am very proud of what we have achieved. For the second year in a row, we have demonstrated that our strategy has revitalized Chr. Hansen so that we not only deliver better results, but we are also producing growth far above industry standards" (press release, www.chr-hansen.com).

To extend its leadership position within cultures and to satisfy the increasing demand particularly for bacterial cultures – a segment with 12–15 percent growth rates in the proceeding years – Chr. Hansen invested approximately DKK 300 million in a new production site at Avedøre, Denmark. During a time where companies were increasingly offshoring

Table 6.3 *Geographical sales development 2006–7*

	2006 gross sales (€ million)	2007 gross sales (€ million)
Europe	254.2	268.3
South America	47	47.8
Asia/Pacific and Middle East	50.6	54.8
North America	128.6	134.6
*Global sales**	480.4	505.5

* Restated excl. excipients.

Source: Chr. Hansen annual accounts

to take advantage of lower production costs, the location choice appeared to run counter to conventional wisdom. However, Denmark was selected as "it is here we have our research and competence center. The Danish educational level is high and it is primarily highly educated professionals we need at the new production site. It is more knowledge than labor intensive" (Lars Frederiksen, *Berlingske Tidende*, October 25, 2007). Lars Frederiksen had every possible reason to be content. The financial situation was promising, fostered by the constructive working relationship between management and PAI. In fact, he had found the process so inspiring and financially sound that he begrudged other Danish companies a similar "dose of medicine." He thought many of them would benefit tremendously from being acquired by a PEF (interview with Lars Frederiksen, January 14, 2008).

Still, some challenges lay ahead. How could Frederiksen diffuse the same set of management mechanisms – accountability, empowerment, sheer determination, and a clear focus – mechanisms that worked so well between PAI and the management group, to all employees in the company? How could he align and internalize objectives and goals across the organization so that employees would feel a personal commitment and would learn to regard the company's goals as theirs as well? During the process, Chr. Hansen had become much more flexible – decision making was quick and implementation was speedy. These attributes were instilled in the management style, but how could they become a more integral part of the corporate culture? Another concern for Frederiksen was how to maintain momentum after PAI's eventual exit. With only two-and-a-half years of PAI ownership and nervous financial markets (as of January 2008), an exit did not constitute an obvious option, at least in the short term. However, he knew one thing for certain: A situation of ownership in limbo could hamstring Chr. Hansen's financial development.

CHR. HANSEN: SUMMARY AND QUESTIONS FOR DISCUSSION

This case study involves what happens to a company when it is acquired by a PEF. It explains the acquisition process and points at opportunities for management innovation when the focus of the company is to become more efficient and prepare for a sale to new owners. Chr. Hansen was put up for sale when its main stakeholder, the Lundbeck Foundation, announced that it no longer intended to be the long-term owner of the controlling equity stake. The French PEF, PAI Partners, acquired the company in 2005, including its headquarters in Hørsholm, and immediately delisted it. PAI planned to continue the growth of Chr. Hansen through geographic expansion, investments in further capacity, R&D, and additional acquisitions. The new CEO, Lars Frederiksen, joined forces with PAI, which he found held a deep level of knowledge and understanding regarding Chr. Hansen's markets. They shared the same vision about the future of Chr. Hansen as they engaged in the implementation of the strategy.

When the PAI team took a closer look at Chr. Hansen, it found that the company had been "under-managed," but that it had a strong human capital potential and a willingness to do things differently within the management group. One of Frederiksen's main tasks was to overcome the myths about the evilness of PEFs and to promote the message internally that private equity ownership could benefit Chr. Hansen and make it possible for it to reach its future objectives. Among other things, Frederiksen emphasized the company's determination to improve performance toward its employees and the opportunities to develop more accountability and better reward systems. The change in ownership led to several drastic changes in the strategy, the organizational setup, the expectations for employee performance, and monitoring via KPIs – all initiatives that held employees at all levels accountable for their actions. The challenge for Frederiksen was to manage this cultural shift from Chr. Hansen's former complacency to an explicit focus on individual contribution and performance, while preparing the entire workforce for PAI's exit at some future point in time. As such, the case facilitates discussion of the following issues:

1. Often PEFs have had a bad press and, for example, a reputation for aggressive tax planning and for not caring about employees and suppliers. CEO Lars

Frederiksen had a different view on this. When PAI Partners acquired Chr. Hansen, it marked the beginning of a journey to reshape the company.

    a. What are the risks involved when shifting from being a listed company to a PEF-owned company?

    b. What are the benefits of working closely with a PEF company? And why can decisions be made faster than in a listed company?

    c. Discuss how Chr. Hansen and PAI worked together? In what ways could it be said that the cooperation was fruitful?

2. Before the takeover, Frederiksen described the company as a sleepy and dusty company where employees were somewhat complacent.

    a. Why was this?

    b. What is meant by "no whip and carrot?"

    c. How should a cultural shift from complacency to an explicit focus on individual accountability and performance be managed?

    d. What was the purpose of introducing PDIs?

3. The shift to private ownership allowed Frederiksen to focus his managerial efforts on the main businesses without short-term pressures from the stock market, the media, and equity analysts. The shift paid off at the management level, but other issues troubled him.

    a. How did the shift affect the employees?

    b. How did he try to get all the employees to buy into the reshaping of the company?

    c. What changes were made in internal communication? Explain the initiatives that were put into action.

4. What will the future bring for Chr. Hansen? How should the organization mentally prepare for PAI's eventual exit (in terms of maintaining focus, momentum, and energy levels)?

    a. What is likely to happen after PAI's eventual exit?

    b. How would momentum be maintained for the employees?

    c. Would it be a good idea for Chr. Hansen to be listed again?

ADDITIONAL SOURCES IN RELATION TO CHR. HANSEN

www.chr-hansen.com

7 IC Companys: Creative genius and commercial attitudes

"This is not the end. It is not even the beginning of the end. But it is, perhaps, the end of the beginning."

Sir Winston Churchill

As he prepared to present the 2006/7 financial results, Henrik Theilbjørn, CEO of the international brand retailer IC Companys, recalled the course of events that had resulted in his appointment to that position in December 2004, following two years as CFO. IC Companys had been established through the merger of two Danish companies, InWear Group and Carli Gry International, in April 2001. Mediocre economic performance in the years following the merger had resulted in a poor working climate and inadequate management capacity. Frustration was widespread. The problems were further exacerbated by tensions among the main shareholders of the company. In his six years with the company, Theilbjørn had watched the situation unfold.

From a revenue perspective, the merger was an "organizational blunder" that had caused substantial annual losses despite the benefits of economies of scale and the elimination of more than 400 redundant employees. The most demotivating factor was, perhaps, the management paralysis that led key people to resign. It was at this moment that a key shareholder and founder of InWear Group, Niels Martinsen, called for an extraordinary general meeting with the sole purpose of installing a new management team. For Theilbjørn, this marked the starting point of a challenging journey to first turn the company around and then unleash the company's growth potential: "We have accomplished the turnaround and are experiencing growth in the majority of our brands and markets. There is a tremendous potential in IC

Companys and I look forward to being part of unleashing that potential in the future" (interview with Henrik Theilbjørn, February 1, 2008).

The 2006/7 numbers made him feel confident and confirmed his optimism. The group's continuing brands experienced a revenue growth of 14 percent, with total revenue reaching DKK 3.353 million, while operating profit (EBIT) increased by 12 percent to DKK 340 million (see Table 7.1). In 2003, when finalizing his MBA studies while also working as CFO, Theilbjørn had set out his ideas for the strategic and organizational platform for IC Companys in his final project. The key was to deploy a multibrand strategy, which encompassed a brand-organized, brand-driven organization structured around individual brands as separate business units. These individual units enjoyed autonomy in brand-building activities such as design, sales, and marketing, which in turn meant dedicated brand teams for the products, sales, and marketing. This was combined with a shared platform to achieve efficiencies through the joint operation of sourcing, distribution, sales logistics, HR, IT, PR, and shop design departments, finance, and administration. Although the strategy seemed to be paying off, Theilbjørn knew he could not rest on his laurels and he was well aware of future challenges that might hamper the company's business model.

First, the decentralized organization in which each label had its own brand director (in principle, a CEO for the brand) highlighted the issues of unity, corporate identity, and subcultures. Theilbjørn's idea was to create a supportive environment via the multibrand/shared platform strategy, giving each brand freedom to develop its own universe and subculture. This freedom could potentially engender feelings of independence. The shared platform strategy entailed evident advantages but also curtailed brand directors' abilities to transact business in some areas. They needed sound arguments and solid business cases vis-à-vis the Executive Board to obtain funds for such activities as line extensions or store rentals. Theilbjørn's job was to keep IC Companys's fashion brands together and ensure that thoughts of secession did not flourish.

Two related issues of concern involved the brand and decentralized organization. The organization around brands resulted in a

Table 7.1 *Financial highlights and key ratios*

	2006/7	2005/6	2004/5	2003/4	2002/3	2001/2	2000/1
Income statement (DKK million)							
Revenue	3,354	3,022	2,821	2,612	2,685	2,891	3,155
Gross profit	1,983	1,768	1,594	1,291	1,437	1,451	1,701
Operating profit before depreciation and amortization	436.4	404	281.6	(76.6)	181.9	–	–
Operating profit before goodwill amortization and special items	342.5	302.5	179.4	(133.3)	121	272.1	274.3
Operating profit before special items	340.1	302.5	179.4	(184)	108.6	136.3	101.2
Operating profit (EBIT)	340.1	322.8	208.6	(275)	44.3	136.3	101.2
Net financial items	(19.7)	(19.9)	(24)	(18.6)	(25.8)	(73.9)	(44.6)
Profit/(loss) before tax	320.4	302.9	184.6	(293.5)	18.5	62.4	(193.5)
Profit/(loss) for the year	240.6	224.4	203	(308.8)	1	42.9	(149.5)
Revenue growth (%)							
Annual growth in revenue	10.9	7.1	8	(2.7)	(7.1)	(8.4)	(3.3)
Cash flows and investments (DKK million)							
Cash flow from operating activities	291.2	326.3	277.9	129.8	183.5	205.5	114.6
Cash flow from investing activities	(186.4)	(141.8)	(82.6)	(77)	(161.5)	(73.5)	(70.8)
Cash flow from operating and investing activities	104.8	184.5	195.3	52.8	22	132	43.8

Table 7.1 (cont.)

	2006/7	2005/6	2004/5	2003/4	2002/3	2001/2	2000/1
Cash flow from financing activities	(261.5)	(163.3)	(3)	22.4	(31.4	(64.1)	(14.9)
Cash flow for the year	(156.7)	21.2	192.3	75.2	(9.5)	67.9	28.9
Key ratios							
Gross margin (%)	59.1	58.5	56.5	49.4	53.5	50.6	53.9
EBITDA margin (%)	13	13.4	10	neg.	6.8	9.3	8.7
EBIT margin (%)	10.1	10.7	7.4	neg.	1.6	4.7	3.2
Return on equity (%)	42	40.1	49.4	neg.	0.2	7.4	neg.
Equity ratio (%)	30.6	34.8	36.6	20.6	33.2	33.2	30.4
Average capital employed including goodwill (DKK million)	1,127	991.6	897	1,037	1,176	1,142	1,256
Return on capital employed (%)	30.4	30.5	20	neg.	10.3	11.9	8.1
Net interest-bearing debt, end of year (DKK million)	557.6	401.9	313.4	496.6	571.6	498.6	611.2
Financial leverage (%)	98.4	69.3	58.2	171.1	95.3	85.5	111.8
Share data							
Market price, end of year (DKK million)	318	344.5	275	42.5	45	35	59.9
Diluted price/earnings (DKK million)	24.5	28.8	24.9	neg.	865.4	14.1	neg.
Employees							
Number of FTEs at the end of the year	2,252	2,032	1,926	2,026	2,344	2,096	2,503
Revenue per FTE (DKK million)	1.489	1.487	1.465	1.289	1.145	1.379	1.260

Source: IC Companys annual reports

number of conflicts between brand and country managers, whose de facto operational room for maneuvering was substantially reduced. The sales responsibility was blurred. For instance, the country managers were not able to set their team (the hire and fire mandate) without consulting the brand managers. The country managers were responsible for the operations in each country; however, their tactical and operational mandate was transferred to the brand managers, which resulted in frustration among the former.

The other related issue involved knowledge sharing across IC Companys's brand portfolio, an aspect that was not strengthened by the decentralized organizational setup. The key question here was how could experiences be shared and best practices disseminated without compromising the authenticity of the brands?

Second, securing continuity in management capacity within the brands constituted a constant challenge. As CEO, Theilbjørn's role could be compared to that of a football coach monitoring and optimizing not one but eleven teams. To be successful, the "players" and directors on each team needed to understand and appreciate the brand, which made it difficult for the CEO to move key employees and management among brand divisions. The issue was how to ensure that the right competences were present in each team to infuse the right sense of commerciality and ownership. How could Theilbjørn pick agile designers with the right commercial instincts and managers who mastered the delicate balance between giving designers the freedom to invent while securing the commercial thread that brought products to the shelves? Essentially, the question was how fashion could be commercialized while keeping complexity under control and still motivating creativity. After all, the design process needed to be based on facts, not just artistic gut feelings!

BACKGROUND

IC Companys is the result of amalgamation and acquisitions of established and upcoming brands. The company is the home of eleven brands that offer fashionable clothing targeting both men and women of various age groups and lifestyle attitudes (see Table 7.2). The

Table 7.2 Brand overview

Output	Background	Peers	Product categories	Growth strategy	Facts
Peak Performance	Peak Performance was established in 1986 and is defined as a mountain resort brand. The brand concept is directed at active people who demand extremely functional products with unique design and uncompromising quality. The brand is positioned in the high-price segment.	The North Face, Patagonia, Helly Hansen, Adidas, and Nike, among others.	Activewear (ski, technical sports, and golf), sportswear (casual, men's and women's), junior, accessories.	The brand will primarily grow through internationalization, an increased focus on sports, junior, and golf wear, and a broader accessories program.	Revenue in 2006/7 grew 24% to DKK 802 million; 39% of revenue was generated outside Scandinavia. The brand has experienced growth in order intake for eighteen collections in a row. Revenue breakdown: 76% wholesale, 22% retail, and 2% outlet.
InWear	InWear was established in 1969. The brand concept is directed at the fashion-conscious	Turnover, Sand, Bruuns Bazaar, Filippa K, and Quiset, among others.	InWear lingerie, accessories, shoes.	The brand will primarily grow through increased penetration of existing markets supported by	Revenue in 2006/7 grew 14% to DKK 540 million; 61% of revenue was generated

Jackpot

Jackpot was established in 1974 and is a lifestyle brand for the modern woman in love with life. A variety of vivid colors and hand-painted patterns characterize a look that will last, with an easy approach to femininity and informality. The brand is positioned as a woman who has a confident and relaxed approach to life, and who is attracted to the cosmopolitan lifestyle. The brand is positioned as "modern" in the upper part of the mid-price segment.

Esprit, Marc O'Polo, Noa Noa, Mexx, Sandwich, and Local Heroes, among others.

Jackpot, Jackpot Girls, Jackpot Home, accessories, shoes.

new retail and franchise stores, along with an increased focus on accessories and the casual part of the collection.

outside Scandinavia. The brand has experienced growth in order intake for six collections in a row. Revenue breakdown: 65% wholesale, 30% retail, and 5% outlet.

The brand will primarily grow through increased penetration of existing markets.

Revenue in 2006/7 fell 11% to DKK 445 million; 80% of revenue was generated outside Scandinavia. The brand experienced a decline in order intake in the winter 2007 collection. Revenue breakdown: 59% wholesale, 35% retail, and 6% outlet.

Table 7.2 (cont.)

Output	Background	Peers	Product categories	Growth strategy	Facts
TIGER OF SWEDEN	Tiger of Sweden was established in 1903. The brand concept is directed at the progressive and fashion-conscious person. The collection is formal, yet with an urban and relaxed attitude and with solid tailoring details. The brand is positioned as "high fashion" in the lower part of the high-price segment. "updated classic" in the mid-price segment.	Hugo Boss, Hugo, Paul Smith, Filippa K, J. Lindeberg, Acne, and Miu Miu, among others.	Black Label, Silver Label, Tiger Jeans, accessories, made-to-order shoes.	The brand will primarily grow through increased internationalization supported by franchise stores.	Revenue in 2006/7 grew 18% to DKK 388 million; 9% of revenue was generated outside Scandinavia. The brand has experienced growth in order intake for more than twenty-three collections in a row. Revenue breakdown: 71% wholesale and 29% retail.
BY MALENE BIRGER	By Malene Birger was established in 2003.	See by Chloé, Marc Jacobs, Vanessa	The Collection, The Salon, accessories.	The brand will primarily grow through	Revenue in 2006/7 grew 40% to DKK 126

	The brand concept is directed at the woman with a taste for uniqueness and exclusiveness. The brand also markets an haute couture line "The Salon." The brand is positioned as "modern" in the high-price segment.	Bruno, Isabel Marant, and Local Heroes, among others.	internationalization and increased penetration of existing markets.	million; 49% of revenue was haute couture outside Scandinavia. The brand has experienced growth in order intake for twelve collections in a row. Revenue breakdown: 88% wholesale and 12% retail.
SOAKED IN LUXURY	Soaked in Luxury was established in 2002. The brand concept is directed at the feminine woman who desires clothes with a touch of overwhelming luxury at a reasonable price. The brand is positioned as a "high street" brand	Vero Moda, B-Young, and Vila, among others.	Soaked in Luxury accessories.	The brand will primarily grow through increased penetration of existing markets supported by new franchise and retail stores.	Revenue in 2006/7 grew 30% to DKK 104 million; 40% of revenue was generated outside Scandinavia. The brand has experienced growth in order intake for two collections in a row. Revenue breakdown:

Table 7.2 (*cont.*)

Output	Background	Peers	Product categories	Growth strategy	Facts
	in the lower part of the mid-price segment.				81% wholesale, 15% retail, and 4% outlet.
DESIGNERS REMIX COLLECTION BY CHARLOTTE ESKILDSEN	Designers Remix Collection was established in 2002. The brand is design-driven and is directed at the female fashion chameleon who desires constant change and clothes with personality. The brand is positioned as "advanced" in the high-price segment.	Bruuns Bazaar, Baum und Pferdgarten and Patrizia Pepe, among others.	Designers Remix Collection, sports and yoga accessories.	The brand will grow through increased penetration of existing markets and new markets.	Revenue in 2006/7 grew 66% to DKK 48 million; 46% of revenue was generated outside Scandinavia. The brand has experienced growth in order intake for ten collections in a row. Revenue breakdown: 72% wholesale, 24% retail, and 4% outlet.
COTTONFIELD EVERYDAY C CLOTHING REG. TRADEMARK	Cottonfield was established in 1986. The brand concept is	Tommy Hilfiger, Gant, Marlboro Classics, Polo, and Ralph	Cottonfield, Cottonfield Female, Cottonfield	The brand will primarily grow through increased penetration of existing	Revenue in 2006/7 grew 18% to DKK 278 million; 68% of

directed at men and women who are attracted to a "U" lifestyle and who demand clothes that make them feel comfortable, relaxed, and sporty. The brand is positioned as "updated casual" in the mid-price segment.

Lauren, among others.

Junior, fragrances, home, shoes.

markets, expansion into China and a female line extension.

revenue was generated outside Scandinavia. The brand has experienced growth in order intake for sixteen collections in a row. Revenue breakdown: 62% wholesale, 32% retail, and 6% outlet.

Matinique

Matinique was established in 1973. The brand concept is directed at the fashion-conscious city man who desires clothes that create a bridge between formal and casual wear. The brand

Sand, Filippa K, Hugo Boss, Hans Ubbink, and Ben Sherman, among others.

City Smart, City Casual, accessories, shoes.

The brand will primarily grow through increased penetration of existing markets.

Revenue in 2006/7 increased 23% to DKK 245 million; 64% of revenue was generated outside Scandinavia. The brand has experienced growth in order intake for eight collections in a row.

Table 7.2 (cont.)

Output	Background	Peers	Product categories	Growth strategy	Facts
	is positioned as "modern" in the upper part of the mid-price segment.				Revenue breakdown: 60% wholesale, 33% retail, and 7% outlet.
PART TWO	Part Two was established in 1986. The brand concept is directed at the fashion-conscious woman who is mentally between twenty-five and twenty-five years of age and demands a unique fashion expression, where the raw and masculine meets the feminine and sensual. The brand is positioned	Sandwich, Noa Noa, Esprit, and Local Heroes, among others.	Part Two accessories.	The brand will primarily grow through increased penetration of existing markets and secondarily through introduction to new markets.	Revenue in 2006/7 increased 13% to DKK 189 million; 49% of revenue was generated outside Scandinavia. The brand has experienced growth in order intake for eight collections in a row. Revenue breakdown: 69% wholesale, 24% retail, and 7% outlet.

SAINT TROPEZ
clothing

	Vila, Vero Moda, and Culture, among others.	Saint Tropez accessories.	The brand will primarily grow through increased penetration of existing markets supported by new franchise stores and an increased focus on in-season sales.	Revenue in 2006/7 fell 6% to DKK 157 million; 29% of revenue was generated outside Scandinavia. Saint Tropez is not a pre-order-based company. Revenue breakdown: 79% wholesale and 21% retail.
as "modern" in the mid-price segment. Saint Tropez was established in 1986. The brand concept is "fast to market" and is directed at the woman who desires high fashion content at a reasonable price. The brand is positioned as "modern" in the lower part of the mid-price segment.				

Source: IC Companys Annual Report, 2006/7

company is one of the largest clothing companies in Northern Europe, with eighteen subsidiaries throughout Europe, Canada, and Hong Kong, and approximately 2,250 employees. The company's sales channels include more than 11,000 wholesale distribution points in more than forty countries, some 220 company-owned shops in thirteen countries, and twenty-one factory outlets. The company's clothing is distributed via wholesale (including franchises) (69 percent), retail (27 percent), and outlet sales (4 percent).

Positioned as a premium brand within active sports, Peak Performance is IC Companys's flagship – and it is growing. While most of the brands experienced growth over the last couple of years, Jackpot, a lifestyle brand "for the modern woman … with an easy approach to femininity and informality," was the Achilles' heel of IC Companys, suffering from declining sales. A new brand director was to reverse this negative development and revitalize the brand. In general, there was a relatively large imbalance in growth and earnings between the original and recently added brands (see Figures 7.1 and 7.2).

IC Companys's brands competed in different market segments and at different price levels, although they had a predominant focus on the middle market. The company did not compete in the very lowest (i.e., hypermarket) or in the highest-priced segments (against brands such as Louis Vuitton). The mid-market segment, valued at approximately €170 billion, was extremely fragmented, with no players holding dominant positions. The mid-market constituted by far the largest segment of the combined fashion market, with annual growth of 2–3 percent (IC Companys's presentation at the Federation of Danish Textile & Clothing's Conference, May 17, 2006).

From a geographical perspective, IC Companys's sales were heavily concentrated in Northern Europe, with approximately half of all sales in the Scandinavian countries (see Table 7.3). Demand for the company's labels was driven by brand identity and image values. Market share per brand was negligible. Together with poor penetration in other European markets and other parts of the world, the company

DKK million	2006/7	2005/6	Growth
Peak Performance	802	646	24%
InWear	540	475	14%
Jackpot	445	499	−11%
Tiger of Sweden	388	328	18%
Cottonfield	278	235	18%
Matínique	245	199	23%
Part Two	189	167	13%
Saint Tropez	157	167	−6%
By Malene Birger	126	90	40%
Soaked in Luxury	104	80	30%
Designers Remix Collection	48	29	66%
Total continuing own brands	**3,322**	**2,915**	**14%**

Source: IC Companys Annual Report, 2006/7

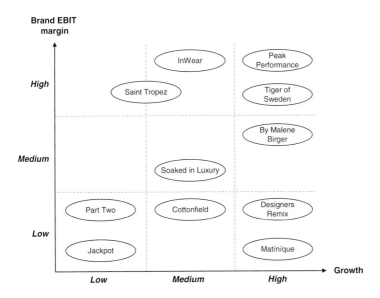

Source: Kaupthing equity research, June 28, 2007

FIGURE 7.1 Revenue by brand, 2006/7, growth, and EBIT margin

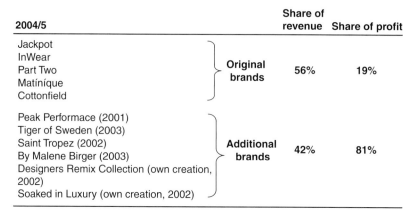

2004/5		Share of revenue	Share of profit
Jackpot InWear Part Two Matíníque Cottonfield	Original brands	56%	19%
Peak Performace (2001) Tiger of Sweden (2003) Saint Tropez (2002) By Malene Birger (2003) Designers Remix Collection (own creation, 2002) Soaked in Luxury (own creation, 2002)	Additional brands	42%	81%

Source: IC Companys Annual Report, 2005/6

FIGURE 7.2 Comparing revenue and profit contribution, 2004/5

saw considerable room for further exploitation of its brand portfolio. Its business strategy involved first and foremost organic growth.

With respect to economic development, IC Companys appeared to have recovered from the unsuccessful merger in 2001 (see Table 7.1) – a merger which was motivated primarily by cost savings. On paper, the merger made good sense. Both companies operated more or less within the same geographical scope and had similar business models selling predominantly through wholesale and retail. Moreover, they produced and sourced in the same countries, so substantial synergies could be obtained from group and sales administration, joint logistics, larger sourcing volumes, and improved rent agreements for retail shops. Annual cost savings were estimated at DKK 125 million, which represented 7–8 percent of the operating cost base at the time (IC Companys Merger Prospectus, 2001). However, from management and brand perspectives, the merger was exceedingly detrimental. For example, Matíníque, a former flagship brand of InWear Group, reported sales of DKK 467.5 million in 1999/2000. In 2004/5, sales of the brand, which bridged formal and casual wear and positioned itself in the upper part of the mid-price segment, amounted to only DKK 200 million.

Table 7.3 *Sales performance by market*

	2006/7 (DKK million)	2005/6 (DKK million)	Growth
Sweden	756	674	12%
Denmark	635	520	22%
Holland	287	274	5%
Norway	276	209	32%
UK and Ireland	180	185	-3%
Belgium	177	154	15%
Finland	167	155	8%
Germany	154	146	6%
Poland	92	88	4%
Canada	90	87	3%
Switzerland	96	84	14%
Spain	71	65	9%
Russia	72	50	44%
Austria	48	46	5%
France	42	36	18%
Other	179	142	26%
Total continuing own brands	**3,322**	**2,915**	**14%**

Source: IC Companys Annual Report, 2006/7

THE RESCUE PLAN

"2004/05 will be the financial year where we will seek to stop the decline and we will see the first signs of improvement in revenue and profit performance" (Henrik Theilbjørn, *Berlingske Nyhedsmagasin*, December 10, 2004). With plummeting sales and profits, as well as weak cash flows, IC Companys found itself suffering a near-death experience. A number of loss-making activities were dismantled, including unprofitable brands (Sir of Sweden and Error) as well as

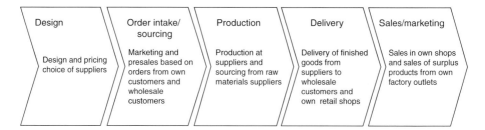

Source: IC Companys Merger Prospectus

FIGURE 7.3   IC Companys value chain

sixty retail stores. While the immediate focus was to "stop the bleed-ing," additional initiatives included the re-establishment of industrial competences, strategic clarification, and a shift in the managerial paradigm. The first of these stressed the need to adopt a more commer-cial approach to all of the company's value chain activities, including design, marketing, purchasing, and sales (see Figure 7.3 for an overview of the value chain).

A commercial approach to design, marketing, sales, and purchasing

One of the more comprehensive initiatives to reinforce commercial awareness and business orientation involved the design process. Historically, IC Companys allowed for a high degree of design compe-tence and the design process functioned relatively independently, without clear commercial goals. Little attention was paid to whether new ideas were actually commercially viable. The problem was that the designers for the acquired declining brands mainly designed clothes that satisfied 20–25 percent of customer demand or the so-called "profile" products in retail stores, which were based on design-ers' interpretation of new trends. However, in a typical retail store, 50 percent of the clothes would be core products and the remaining 25 percent would be basic styles (see Figure 7.4). In response to this artistic, "gut feeling"-based approach to design, a more fact-based,

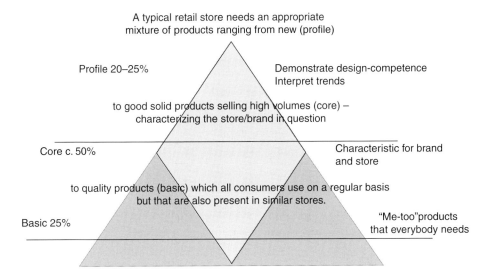

Source: IC Companys presentation to Dansk Tekstil Beklædning, 2006

FIGURE 7.4 Style composition in fashion clothing design

systematic, and commercial planned design process was introduced. Designers and product developers had to interpret consumer mindsets and preferences, including such factors as the number of "choices" a consumer made per square meter in retail stores as well as what designs would sell. In order to better reflect demand, systematized sales reviews of former collections and improved market feedback served as critical inputs for future collections. The collection structure was further tightened to include only four main collections with some color variations, reflecting an appropriate mix between profile, core, and basic clothing products.

With respect to marketing, initiatives sought to make campaigns and messages more commercially supportive from a commercial angle. Previously, the marketing function had focused on building and nurturing an image, which makes perfect sense for such luxury brands as Gucci or Prada, but not for IC Companys, which first and foremost wanted to sell its clothing products to customers who desired high-quality items at competitive prices. Moreover, during the merger, the company attempted to centralize purchasing for its own retail stores, but this move failed because the necessary IT tools were not in place. With a more integrated IT platform, purchasing was centralized in 2005 – this time with better results.

Another initiative to become more commercially driven involved IC Companys's outlet division. Selling surplus products from the main sales channels (wholesale, franchise, and retail), the outlet activities only comprised 5 percent of the company's revenue, but they served as an important element in the strategy to become more brand-oriented. The company's business model typically implied a 5–10 percent surplus from any one collection. Outlets had previously been regarded as "garbage cans" in which surplus clothes could be dropped. However, according to Henrik Theilbjørn, this perception needed to change if attempts to professionalize this division were to succeed. In his mind, outlets were the same as retail, just one season later. This perception prompted a more prudent approach in order to protect brand value. A new sorting and picking inventory facility in Poland was established to supply the company's twenty-one outlets in nine countries. Although the company constantly worked to reduce the inflow of surplus products (via higher penalties for returning unsold goods), the division contributed DKK 23 million in profit and had a profit margin of 17.5 percent in 2006/7.

Strategic clarification: Brand-driven management structure

To reinforce organizational empowerment and accountability, as well as to restore motivation and ambition, management saw its multi-brand strategy as key. It wanted accountable, team-based leaders with the courage of their convictions: "I hate official acts and I hate negligence … I need strong people around me to help me make the right decisions. In that way, it is important that the organization is responsible – that it commits itself and takes a stand whether things are good or bad. If you just pass on papers, you are simply a public servant" (Henrik Theilbjørn, *Børsen*, December 2, 2005).

Each brand worked as an independent company, which was headed by a brand director with bottom-line responsibility. Each brand had bonus schemes linked to performance. This ensured dedicated management for each brand. The overriding tasks of the brand divisions were to build, position, and develop the brand. Their objective was to increase brand equity – to use the brand as a platform to launch related products or enhance consumer attitudes toward products associated with the brand. The brand divisions were also responsible for the design process, sourcing, and marketing. It was critical for building brand equity and credibility that brand directors and employees were brand champions capable of "living the brand" in all their activities. For some brands, this worked exceptionally well, while others suffered a more faltering course. Stability and continuity in management and key employees were critical in this respect.

Jonas Ottosson, Brand Director for Peak Performance, served as a prominent example of how the brand and its director were inseparable. Peak Performance was acquired by Carli Gry International in 1998 and merged with IC Companys in 2001. Having been with the company for nineteen years, Ottosson's lifestyle was synonymous with the brand's main characteristics: Active, outdoor, and sporty. In addition to the weekly running trips and mountain bike rides in which he found his inspiration, he was a skilled skier and golfer. In contrast, Matíníque's erratic course following the merger had moved the brand away from its core, confusing the wholesale segment and end-users. However, with a new brand director and chief designer in place, the brand managed to revitalize itself after 2005.

According to IC Companys, the multibrand strategy allowed it to diversify risks. The company profiled brands with high fashion content and launched a minimum of four collections a year with long lead times. Correctly predicting consumer tastes and preferences was essential to success. In order to reduce risk, each brand implemented the commercial and fact-based development of its collections.

The Executive Board, consisting of Henrik Theilbjørn and COO Mikkel Vendelin Olesen, met five to six times a year with all brand directors to discuss status, strategy, and budgets. Theilbjørn was responsible for five brands, including Peak Performance and Tiger of Sweden, while Vendelin Olesen closely monitored most of the original brands, including Part Two, Matínique, and Jackpot. Both of them met on a regular basis with their responsible brand directors to discuss strategic challenges (see Figure 7.6b). Reporting was standardized and followed a simple KPI framework, which enabled executive management to monitor the decentralized business activities. In addition, the framework allowed brand directors to present strategic considerations in a structured, concise manner. With the help of external consultants, methods and processes were occasionally updated and fine-tuned without compromising brand identity, innovation, or creativity.

While the multibrand organization concentrated power around the brand directors who reported directly to top management, the decision-making power of a local country manager was heavily reduced. The country manager position was maintained during the organizational transformation, but in reality such managers could not take tactical and operational decisions without consulting the brand managers. They had bottom-line responsibility and were measured on KPIs, some of which they were unable to influence or control. In that sense, the power balance in the matrix (brands and geographies) became somewhat distorted.

Shared platform

The brands were backed by a shared platform that allowed for the realization of sizeable synergies in the supply chain and in other joint corporate functions such as IT, sales logistics, finance, HR, and administration (see Figure 7.5). Approximately 550 employees worked on the basis of the shared platform. According to Theilbjørn, the business model was pivotal to the company's competitiveness, as it created considerable cost efficiencies for each brand, regardless of size, through lower sourcing costs. As sourcing activities were pooled, all brands were better able to respond to sudden geographical changes and to exploit new sourcing opportunities. In addition, the shared platform

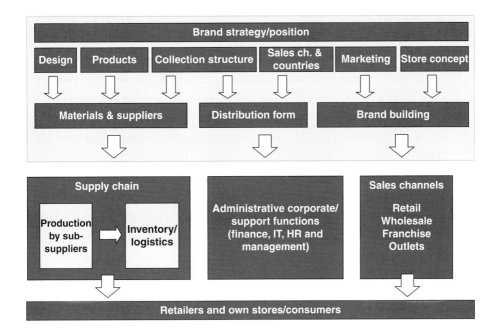

Source: IC Companys Annual Report, 2004

FIGURE 7.5 Dividing lines between the shared platform and brand activities

ensured more stable deliveries to retailers and the company's concept stores. Finally, the IT backbone worked as the glue that linked activities in production, sales logistics, and administration. For example, when the company launched a loyalty program in 2007 to strengthen brand loyalty and increase sales per customer within selected brands, IT played a critical role. While the brands involved in this designed and fine-tuned the specific shape and content of the program, the supporting technological (IT) backbone was designed at the corporate level to ensure scale effects and ease future roll-outs.

The multibrand strategy enabled IC Companys to handle a number of strong, distinct brands with clear profiles. At the same time, the company aimed to develop a scalable "plug and play" structure via the shared platform, which would enable the integration of future brand acquisitions at a lower cost and ensure the efficient management of existing brands. The flagship brand, Tiger of Sweden, serves as a case in point. Prior to the integration of Tiger in 2002, the brand had revenues of DKK 190 million and a 7 percent profit ratio. In 2004/5, sales amounted to DKK 300 million and the profit ratio was 14 percent.

The dividing line between the shared platform and the brand activities has changed over time as it is not always clear where the different activities should be located. At one end of the scale, we have design, product development, and sales, which are clearly brand-specific activities, while at the other end of the scale, we have more generic administrative activities like finance, IT, and HR, which obviously can be handled across the brands. However, there are then a number of activities in the gray zone between the two ends of the scale like marketing and sourcing. Over the years, IC Companys has experimented with how to best organize marketing activities. Currently it works on disaggregating the marketing activities, so those that are more brand-specific will be located with the brands while other marketing activities will be taken care of in the shared platform. A similar development can be seen for the sourcing activities, where each brand has its own team in the larger sourcing and production units abroad. This exercise is all about reaping the benefits of economies of scale without destroying the uniqueness of each brand.

Another area where IC Companys is constantly fine-tuning the organization is when it comes to the payment of the services in the shared platform. It is not mandatory for the brands to use the shared platform, but the ambition is obviously to make it as attractive for all brands to use as many of the services from the platform as possible. However, the fact is that not all brands use all the services offered; in particular, some of the recently acquired brands use the shared platform to a lesser extent. Before the brands were all paying a fixed share of the turnover for all the services in the shared platform, but as the use of the services varies among the brands and since the requirements for the qualities of the demanded services vary, the company has started to introduce a system of fair fee payment. One example is in packaging where it is much cheaper if clothes are flat-packed, while those brands that require more sophisticated packaging like jackets on hangers need to pay more (i.e., a fair fee).

New management paradigm and HR upgrade

Erratic changes in strategy, coupled with intense turbulence among the owners following the merger in 2001, had made employees despondent. After experiencing years of decline, many employees felt demotivated. Ambitions and a winner mentality were not concepts in the company's vocabulary, and the management was afraid of committing errors. A key priority for Henrik Theilbjørn, following his appointment as CEO, was to give more managerial and financial attention to the HR function: "Our ability to develop mid-level managers and leaders calls for improvement, and the same goes for internal recruitment and retaining talent. I do not believe you can be successful solely via external recruits. Typically, it takes some months for the person to settle and then it takes [an] additional 6–12 months for training and education. That means a loss of valuable time. We may not be able to recruit internally in all cases, but we need to be more active in the area" (*Børsen*, August 11, 2006).

Using HR strategically within fashion was not often a priority. However, following the introduction of the multibrand strategy, IC Companys pinpointed HR as a key focus area that could drive retail sales, enhance leadership development, and strengthen talent management efforts. In 2006, Ditte Marstrand, an HR executive with twelve years of experience with such companies as Microsoft, was hired to build up an international HR organization in which the number of HR employees would be doubled to eighteen. The plan was to establish four academies (leaders, sales, retail, and brands) and to work more actively with employee development.

The decentralized, autonomous brand structure obscured a consistent overview of leadership and talent capacity, which made it difficult to secure continuity by offering new positions to talented employees at all levels. As a main catalyst, the new HR function conducted reviews and provided a platform for employee development, internal recruitment, and succession planning. These initiatives improved internal planning, created awareness about internal career paths, and, consequently, strengthened the company's ability to retain talented employees. The close monitoring of employee development and the focus on internal career opportunities were aimed at increasing the share of internal recruits to leading positions. In addition, a strong focus on HR and internal opportunities gave management credibility. As Ditte Marstrand stated: "It sends a strong signal internally when we communicate that an appointed retail manager has worked as [a] sales assistant for a number of years in another retail store" (*Børsen*, August 11, 2006).

A natural consequence of having eleven independent brands was that there was a bottleneck in management capacity. In consequence, the idea behind the Leadership Academy, established in 2007, was to develop basic leadership competences and execution, while equipping managers with tools to develop their teams. The task was quite extensive, as 200 of the company's middle managers had never been offered leadership training. Moreover, a top assessment of management was conducted to evaluate competences and identify strengths and development areas. To play down possible apprehensions and to add legitimacy to the exercise, Henrik Theilbjørn was the first to be "tested."

Also important was the setup of a retail academy aimed at developing and standardizing the competences in the retail division. The education and training of 900 retail staff members were seen as key to achieving higher revenue per square meter in the retail stores.

All of these initiatives helped to streamline IC Companys by imposing a more prudent commercial discipline on all aspects of its business operations – from the initial idea to the shelf in the store. Moreover, it marked the first steps toward establishing an organization in which accountability, motivation, and a team-based performance culture were emphasized. The move from a functional focus to a brand focus helped to decentralize the decision-making process and make brand divisions fully responsible for their economic performance (see Figure 7.6). In retrospect, Theilbjørn commented: "The easy part is a

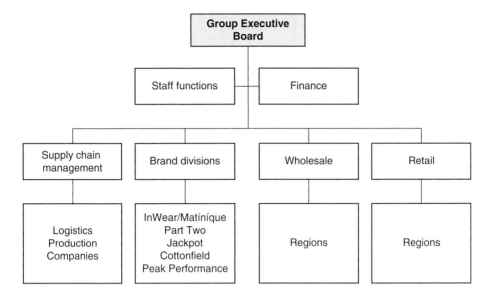

Source: IC Companys Annual Report, 2003

FIGURE 7.6A Former organizational structure

turnaround. When you are standing next to the coffin with the cover in your hand, you are, effortlessly, able to mobilize a common understanding and sense of urgency. Now it is time to show that we can develop the company and stick to a long term strategy. The new motivation has to come from raising the level of ambition" (*Magasinet Lederne*, no. 2, February, 2008). However, the execution of the multibrand strategy did encounter some challenges.

DEFINING DIVIDING LINES AND RESPONSIBILITIES

One inherent dilemma was to define the exact boundaries in terms of the roles, responsibilities, and contractual agreements between the corporate functions and brand divisions. In principle, the management of each brand was responsible for all activities that formed part of that brand's identity (i.e., everything visible to the customer). Each brand

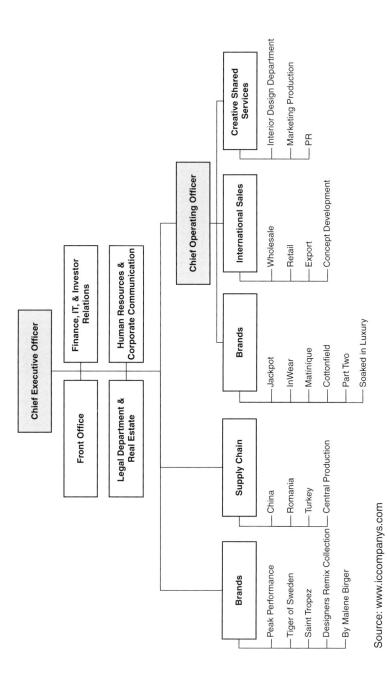

Source: www.iccompanys.com

FIGURE 7.6B Current organizational structure

had formalized service level agreements (SLAs) with the joint function center and paid a service fee for the use of its services, typically a percentage of turnover. However, the level of the service fee deviated substantially among brands. More autonomous brands, like Peak Performance and Tiger of Sweden, were not subject to the same mechanisms or rules as the original brands (see Figure 7.6b). The original brands generally paid a relatively high service fee, while recently acquired or self-created brands benefitted from a less harsh fee policy. The SLAs specified the content and scope of the services offered, but they were difficult to broaden sufficiently to accommodate all the needs of the brands, which caused frustration among brand directors at times. Brand managers could discuss their discontent with group management to improve procedures, but essentially they could not buy their services externally. Another issue involved internal invoicing between brands. Upcoming brands often profited from the original brands' knowledge concerning such aspects as store location in foreign markets. This kind of knowledge sharing benefitted the company as a whole, but how could this kind of assistance be charged for when, for instance, a Cottonfield or Matíníque country manager used a day to identify attractive store locations for an upcoming brand?

One issue was contractual agreements. Another was to identify when activities or responsibilities ended or coalesced in some instances. Traditionally, marketing had been centralized, but it had proven difficult to meet the specific requirements of brand divisions or to capture the characteristics of each brand. In one instance, the Brand Director of Matíníque, Claus Bendixen, had found his Christmas card design in London and handed it over to the central marketing department. The card expressed the values Matíníque wanted to convey in a compelling way. Therefore, when he found his Christmas card used for all of IC Companys's brands with color as the only distinct feature, the concept was watered down. He explained: "Obviously, the joint functions seek standardization to minimize costs, but when it comes to marketing, it is difficult to have a 'one size fits all' approach. The ultimate aim of marketing is to keep the distinctiveness of each brand and not to standardize. Marketing does not always fit into the fixed structure, the shared platform and SLAs, represent" (interview with Claus Bendixen, March 7, 2008). Part of the marketing function was decentralized in 2007, giving the brand divisions more latitude. The joint marketing function maintained responsibility for more general areas, such as marketing materials and interior design (shop concepts), while the creative activities were transferred to the brands.

Packaging was another area in which lines were blurred. The fact that some brands required more exclusive packaging and careful handling when transported threatened to neutralize the benefits of economies of scale in transportation and logistics. These additional costs, associated with expressing brand identity, needed to be justified in one way or another. This could, for instance, involve using hangers for suits or putting a personal card in each customer box prior to shipment to retail stores.

Henrik Theilbjørn dwelled for a moment on the journey of the past five years. In his view, in the beginning IC Companys had tried to conform to the golden rule in fashion: *Don't ask consumers what they want – tell them what they should have*. However, according to his own rule of thumb, when selling clothes primarily to the upper part of the mid-market, design and product development practices needed to be based on a specific ratio: 70 percent facts and 30 percent gut feelings. In other words, what was needed was a fine mixture of good business sense and intuition. This had important implications for the competences and management capacity present in each brand division. Each brand needed managers who were respectful of the creative process and designers with strong commercial instincts.

At a corporate level, Theilbjørn needed to maintain IC Companys as a whole, balancing structure and scope with creativity. In particular, the delegation of mandates and decision rights between brands and country managers had to be optimized. Furthermore, each brand director had to buy into the idea of a multibrand strategy on a shared platform (IC Companys's *raison d'être*). It was also necessary for the directors to cultivate and appreciate the specific brand's subcul-ture – an exercise not always aligned with corporate concerns. The job was to future-proof the company's position as a home of fashion brands while ensuring that internal power struggles could not gain a foothold. In addition, methods had to be identified to allow best practices and experiences to be shared among brands without eroding brand equity.

While the financial turnaround had been successful, the organ-izational redesign was more problematic. However, Theilbjørn felt confident. A number of growth initiatives had been launched aimed at long-term transformation, including the revitalization of the origi-nal brands, the remodeling of concept stores and line extensions, and the company was generally on the right track. Together with the COO and the Board, new financial targets had been outlined. Over a period of three to five years, the target was to achieve minimum annual organic growth of 15 percent and an EBIT margin of a minimum of 15 percent (IC Companys Annual Report, 2006/7). No, the journey had definitely not ended. It had barely begun!

IC COMPANYS: SUMMARY AND QUESTIONS FOR DISCUSSION

IC Companys was founded in April 2001 through a merger of InWear Group A/S and Carli Gry International. The company experienced a difficult period after the merger and several years passed before a satisfying performance was achieved. The difficulties consisted of both managerial and economic challenges. Since then, the company has changed its strategy and has continuously innovated with regard to its management practices, which together have contributed to the improved results. Being in the fashion and clothing business, IC Companys is a cyclical company that is affected to a signficant degree by economic fluctuations. It operates in a highly competitive market where differentiation is of the utmost importance. It has developed a multibrand strategy, where all brands are marketed in the mid- and high-end price segment. This multibrand strategy, combined with a shared business platform, has made it possible to simultaneously increase the focus on brand differentiation, customer loyalty, economies of scale, and a reduction in costs. Over the years, IC Companys has step-by-step fine-tuned the workings of the multibrand strategy (which entails the uniqueness of each brand) and the shared business platform (which entails the standardization of back-office activities).

In 2004, IC Companys appointed Henrik Theilbjørn as CEO after a two-year period as CFO. Looking back at the merger and the installment of a new management team Theilbjørn describes the challenging journey from turning the company around to unleashing the company's growth potential. He created the multibrand strategy and initiated a redesign of the organization aligned with the brands, which encompassed a brand-driven organization structured around individual brands as separate business units combined with the shared platform. This strategy has paid off financially, but the organizational redesign turned out to be more problematic. The job was to future-proof the company's position as a home of fashion brands while ensuring that internal struggles would not result in self-destructive turf wars and subcultures that were too autonomous. Another area of focus for the future was to identify a way to share best practices and experiences among brands without eroding brand uniqueness. As such, the case facilitates discussion of the following issues:

1. IC Companys was founded as a result of a merger. The merger turned out to be an "organizational blunder" and a significant amount of damage control was needed. Synergies needed to be rebuilt and new roles and responsibility needed to be divided.
   a. What are the core competences of IC Companys? Define and evaluate its core competences after the merger.
   b. In what position is the company's competitive situation after the merger?
   c. What is the composition of the company's product portfolio in relation to future earnings?
2. IC Companys was a decentralized organization, where each label had its own brand director. Henrik Theilbjørn wanted to create a supportive environment that would give each brand more freedom and a chance to develop its own universe and subculture.

    a. What were the two major issues concerning the brand-focused and decentralized organization?

    b. What caused the frustration among the country managers?

    c. How could experiences be shared and best practices disseminated without compromising the uniqueness of the brands?

3. What initiatives were made to keep complexity under control and still motivate creativity?

    a. Explain the multibrand strategy.

    b. Theilbjørn's role as a CEO is compared to a football coach: Why is this?

    c. Explain how management went from "gut feeling" to a more fact-based orientation?

4. The multibrand organization centered power around the brand directors who reported directly to top management. The decision-making power of a local country manager was heavily reduced as a consequence. How did this affect the matrix structure?

    a. Explain "plug and play."

    b. Theilbjørn preferred to keep the recruiting process internal. What are the pros and cons of doing this?

    c. Why did Theilbjørn want to dedicate more managerial and financial attention to HR?

    d. How did top management balance the employee mix between commercial and creative skillsets (creative managers and commercialized designers)?

ADDITIONAL SOURCES IN RELATION TO IC COMPANYS

www.iccompanys.com

Reeslev, C. K. (2009), *En rebel bliver børsnoteret: En fortælling om Niels Martinsen, InWear og IC Companys*. Copenhagen: Gyldendal Business.

8   NKT Flexibles: Global sourcing of R&D innovation

Sitting in his office, the R&D Manager of NKT Flexibles, Niels Rishøj, took a break, turned his chair around, and looked out the window. As a flock of birds passed by in the sky, he considered the challenge he faced. In recent years, NKT Flexibles had been very successful in producing and selling complex, high-quality flexible pipe systems for a number of offshore oil and gas applications. Turnover had grown from approximately US$98 billion in 2005 to US$280 billion in 2008 (Table 8.1). This growth was largely a result of the company's focus on innovation. It had no doubts that continued innovation was of key importance if it was to remain competitive.

Behind Rishøj, a PowerPoint presentation on the pros and cons of open innovation was open on his PC. In preparation for the introduction of a new strategy, the Board had asked him to make recommendations on the innovation strategy. He had almost finalized the presentation, but one slide remained – his final recommendations. Overall, he was quite pleased with the results of the current innovation strategy, but his experience told him that there was still room for improvement and beneficial modifications. He reconsidered all aspects of the innovation strategy, repeatedly asking himself "What have we learned and where can we make improvements?"

The main inspiration for the current innovation strategy had been the concept of open innovation. NKT Flexibles was too small to conduct proper research in every technological area in which it needed state-of-the-art expertise, so from the outset the company had collaborated with others. Rishøj felt that "we couldn't exist on the market if we didn't have the option of drawing on all these others to help us … we would not be able to sufficiently renew ourselves."

Table 8.1 *Financial key figures for NKT Flexibles (US$ million)*

	2009	2008	2007	2006	2005
Annual revenue	238.7	279.4	247.4	176.8	98.2
Operational EBITDA	55.5	92.6	53.8	27.6	10.6
Operational EBIT	47.5	85.6	47.4	21.2	5.0
Capital employed	141.9	111.2	82.6	55.8	62.6
Tangible asset investments	n.a.	20.8	19.6	10.4	4.4
Average number of employees	490*	571	474	356	264

* Number of employees as of December 31.

Source: Annual reports. All figures based on the author's currency calculations

Unquestionably, the open innovation strategy had served the company well. However, the benefits of collaborating with external partners came at a price. Such collaborative partnerships created some dilemmas, such as the need to explain to internal R&D staff that external partners might be better at innovation in some areas. More importantly, the open innovation strategy left the company with less control over the R&D process. Although open innovation allowed it to tap into others' expert knowledge, it entailed the danger that NKT Flexibles would become dependent on external knowledge. Rishøj wondered how the company could achieve the right balance between internal and external sources of innovation.

The birds had disappeared, leaving nothing but the evening twilight in the sky. Rishøj knew he had to finalize the presentation by the end of the day, but his feelings were still mixed. He had yet to make up his mind about the recommendation he would make.

INTRODUCING NKT FLEXIBLES

Following its foundation in 1891, *Aktieselskabet Nordiske Kabel- og Traadfabrikker*, now known as NKT Holding, was in an almost constant state of change. Over the years, NKT Holding had grown into a conglomerate of four different firms that produced and sold a wide variety of products all over the world. The four firms were: *NKT Cables*, which produced and sold power cables for the electricity and energy sectors; *Nilfisk Advance*, which supplied professional cleaning equipment; *NKT Photonics*, which produced and sold fiber-based measuring equipment and light sources; and *NKT Flexibles*, which produced and sold flexible pipe systems for the offshore oil and gas industry.

The flexible pipe systems developed by NKT Flexibles were used for mixed flexible and rigid solutions, and for wholly flexible field developments in dynamic environments, such as the sea. The different kinds of pipe systems served different purposes: *Flowlines* were used to carry fluids on the sea bed, *risers* connected floating production vessels (known as FPSOs) to the sub-sea infrastructures, *jumpers* connected two fixed/floating structures either above or below water, and *fluid transfer lines* were large-diameter pipes connecting two (often dynamic) structures.

Since its first installation of a flexible pipe system off the coast of Iceland in 1968, NKT Flexibles had broadened the range of environments in which its pipe systems could be used to encompass not only near-coastal shallow waters but also ultra-deepwaters. At the same time, the company expanded the pressure and temperature ratings of its products providing broad-based expertise in flexible pipe solutions for the offshore oil and gas industry. By 2008, it was capable of delivering pipe systems that maintained their flexibility at pressures of up to 600 bars and resisted temperatures of up to 130°C. NKT Flexible's pipes consisted of several different layers of plastic and steel (Figure 8.1), which ensured a high degree of flexibility in the pipe. Not only could the different layers be altered to meet customer requirements, but the size of the pipe could also be changed – from two to sixteen inches in diameter – depending on the customer's needs.

NKT Flexibles developed its expertise in technological niches via its focus on R&D. It successfully differentiated itself from competitors

1. Carcass
An interlocking structure manufactured from a metallic strip. The carcass prevents collapse of the inner liner and provides mechanical protection against pigging tools and abrasive particles.

2. Inner liner
An extruded polymer layer providing internal fluid integrity.

3. Pressure armor
A number of structural layers consisting of helically wound C–shaped metallic wires and/or metallic strips. The pressure armor layers provide resistance to radial loads.

4. Tensile armor
A number of structural layers consisting of helically wound flat metallic wires. The layers are counter wound in pairs.

5. Outer sheath
An extruded polymer layer. The function is to shield the pipe's structural elements from the outer environment and to provide mechanical protection.

Source: www.nktflexibles.com
FIGURE 8.1 Example of a pipe construction

within such segments as high-temperature pipe applications and was able to offer cost-effective solutions because of its ability to understand and improve the properties of polymeric and metallic materials. Furthermore, it could compete in riser-integrity management services with a range of products that incorporated the use of optical fiber technology. The company's design principles, combined with its novel production methods, were the key to maintaining a zero-target failure statistic for its products in service. Furthermore, its in-house system of analysis competence made it a preferred supplier for shallow water projects, where the often severe movements of riser systems were a challenge for customers in terms of maintaining system integrity.

The move toward Flextreme

NKT Flexibles had recently expanded its competence in temperature monitoring to the monitoring of metal fatigue in pipes through the use of optical fibers that were placed into the pipes' steel construction. As Niels Rishøj indicated, "we produce a little gadget, which can take some laser-based measurements. What makes it really interesting when we talk offshore oil and gas production is ... that you can place this equipment in areas on a platform, which are susceptible to being surrounded by hydrocarbon vapors. [This is important as] there is a risk of explosion in those areas and consequently, you cannot easily place anything electric there." NKT Flexibles was the only flexible pipe system supplier that offered this type of advanced monitoring system, which allowed for online monitoring of the steel's tension, thereby minimizing the risk of metal fatigue failures and assisting in the timely pipe replacements, if required.

Another focus area was ultra-deepwater (typically depths of more than 1,500–2,000 meters) research. Historically, oil extraction had been executed on land or offshore in relatively shallow water depths of less than 500 meters. However, as the amount of untapped oil reserves began to decline, the demand for developing equipment to bring oil and gas from deep and ultra-deepwater fields to the surface increased. Therefore, many of NKT Flexibles's R&D resources were focused on further product innovation within deep and ultra-deepwater pipe systems. The decision to concentrate on this type of product led to the innovation of an entirely new concept of flexible pipe system, which was the Flextreme concept.

The Flextreme concept was based on utilizing fiber-reinforced materials like carbon fibers, as such fibers were more suitable for deepwater products than the conventional metal-based pipes being offered by NKT Flexibles. At that point, carbon fibers were the most obvious material choice that could handle the extreme conditions experienced in deepwater. In order to develop this product line, the company needed access to the latest knowledge on carbon fiber technology, which would be too cumbersome for the company to develop by itself. It began to look for potential partners for knowledge sharing.

Logistics

NKT Flexibles worked with many suppliers of steel, plastic, and raw materials, as well as suppliers of semi-constructed parts. It prioritized finding the right balance among all of its suppliers – not only were there many of them, but they were often located internationally, which created a number of challenges. For NKT Flexibles, putting the value chain puzzle together and delivering the product to its customers in time was sometimes a challenge.

Located on the coast at Kalundborg, Denmark, NKT Flexibles's production site had its own harbor side, which allowed the factory to ship products directly to the customers. In fact, a location on the coast was necessary, as the final product – pipe spooled on huge reels – could only be transported by ship. In addition, the location of the production site 90 km from headquarters and the testing centre in Copenhagen had certain advantages in terms of communication. Rishøj indicated that "a strong dialogue with the factory is very important. We have several issues on different levels every day that we need to solve together with the factory."

Market and customers

Market trends for flexible pipe systems followed the developments in the oil and gas industry. It had an average market size of US$1.5 billion per year and analysts expected it to grow to US$2.5 billion in 2013. NKT Flexibles held a market share of approximately 15 percent and was one of only three flexible offshore pipe system manufacturers in the world (Table 8.2). The company's main competitors were the French company *Technip*, with a market share of 55 percent, and the British company *Wellstream*, with a market share of 30 percent. In comparison to these two competitors, NKT Flexibles was more of a niche company. Technip was a "total-solution" company that supplied complete pipe systems, including the offshore installation of these. The fact that it operated in three different business segments – sub-sea, offshore, and onshore – meant that it had a much wider

Table 8.2 *Competitors*

	Technip	Wellstream	NKT Flexibles
Employees	23,000	1,000+	600+
Plants	France (HQ), Brazil	UK (HQ), Brazil, USA	Denmark (HQ)
Amount invested in R&D	US$20.2 billion	Data not available	Data not available
Market share	55%	30%	15%
Revenue (2008/2007)	US$3,672 billion/ US$3,384 billion*	US$566 billion/ US$408 billion	US$279 billion/ US$247 billion
Gross margin (2008/2007)	US$971 billion/ US$762 billion	US$177 billion/ US$119 billion	US$85 billion/ US$49 billion
Operating profit (2008/ 2007)	US$714 billion/ US$532 billion	US$122 billion/ US$71 billion	US$79 billion/ US$44 billion

* Financial figures represent the sub-sea segment of Technip.

Source: Annual reports and websites. All currency figures based on the author's currency calculations

product portfolio. In contrast, Wellstream focused on fast delivery and large volumes of more standardized flexible pipe systems.

NKT Flexibles's main customers were large oil companies, including Statoil, BP, Shell, Petrobras, Exxon Mobil, Maersk, and Total, along with several specialized entrepreneurs, such as APL, SBM, and Blue Water. Given its customers' activities, the company had business and projects spread across the world.

Approximately 50 percent of the market for flexible pipe systems was located in the Atlantic Ocean off the Brazilian coast. The other half of the market was divided amongst West Africa, the North Sea, the Gulf of Mexico, the Far East, and Australia. In 2008, NKT Flexibles won a three-year contract with the Brazilian oil company Petrobras. At the same time, Petrobras was planning its future investments in offshore oil extraction in deepwater, which would be good news for NKT Flexibles if it could become Petrobras's preferred supplier. Therefore, innovation and development in deep and ultra-deepwater flexible pipe systems was more important than ever. Rishøj knew that innovation and the ability to handle complex projects were vital to attracting large customers like Petrobras.

INNOVATION AND R&D OUTSOURCING

From the start, NKT Flexibles outsourced large parts of its value chain. Some parts were obvious targets for outsourcing, such as the supply of steel and other raw materials, while others seemed less relevant for outsourcing, such as some of the innovation activities. However, it soon became clear that NKT Flexibles's "invent-it-ourselves" model of innovation was incapable of sustaining high levels of growth. The company could not conduct state-of-the-art research in all of the technology areas in which it needed expertise. Therefore, it had to draw on the innovations of others. Instead of only having the company as the "innovation market," it was decided that the innovation market would be the whole world.

However, the company had no intention of outsourcing core competences, although the perception of what constituted core competences changed over time. As Niels Rishøj reflected, "that what we exactly call our core competency changes with time. Our core competency ten years ago was different from what it is today." Most of the time, this strategy meant that NKT Flexibles was outsourcing innovation activities for which external partners already had the required competence, but sometimes it decided to bring some innovation activities back in-house to create its own competencies because some important knowledge was lost in the process of outsourcing. The decision over what to outsource and what to keep internally reflected a learning process in which the boundaries had to be continually adjusted to reflect the new requirements for innovation and to ensure that the company had the best access to innovation.

One case serves to illustrate these changes in boundaries. Early on, NKT Flexibles did not possess the necessary competencies to make dynamic calculations of its pipe systems and it therefore decided to outsource that activity. However, the company soon realized that it was crucial for the system engineers handling the dynamic calculations to be able to quickly and easily communicate with the engineers constructing the pipes early on in the process. Early communication was important because it was much cheaper to make adjustments while the product plans were still on the drawing board than to make adjustments after the pipe was in production. Consequently, the dynamic calculation activity was brought back in-house and grew into one of NKT Flexibles's key competences.

NKT Flexibles has many external supplier partners. "Basically, for every layer in the flexible pipe, we have at least one partner – and normally more than one," said Rishøj. According to him, the extensive sourcing strategy not only benefitted NKT Flexibles but also provided strong incentives for the partners in most cases: "They can see it is good business in the long run and that's why they go to their labs and run development projects at their own cost. But there are other cases where we decide to pay [for a partner] to conduct the development project, as they would not do so otherwise."

The open innovation strategy provided NKT Flexibles with access to more knowledge than it could have generated itself. However, it was not easy for the company to handle having the whole world as its knowledge base. It constantly faced difficult decisions regarding which areas of in-house R&D to expand. Experience had shown that it was very important to keep knowledge on the design and architecture of the system as a whole – the knowledge of how the different pieces in the system fit together – in-house, while it was advantageous to outsource some of the pieces that had clear, specific interfaces with other elements in the flexible pipe system.

In addition to the knowledge development aspect, there were several other reasons to outsource R&D activities to external partners that had better or more specialized expertise. At times, the outsourcing of R&D gave rise to additional advantages, such as more favorable tax situations, lower salaries, or a more standardized R&D process. Furthermore, the outsourcing of R&D could result in a faster time to market, a transfer of technology, or access to a new market.

Rishøj had experienced all of these benefits during his time with the company – benefits he was reluctant to relinquish. However, the benefits also came at a price, as the company risked losing control of outsourced resources and core competencies. The outsourcing of R&D might come at the expense of unintentional transfer of core technology and the loss of in-house competencies, or might even result in the damage of intellectual property rights. In addition, there were the in-house R&D staff members to be considered – they might lose their motivation if most of the challenging R&D projects were outsourced. Finally, the outsourcing of R&D inevitably meant a higher degree of dependency on the external partners.

NKT Flexibles had already addressed some of these risks. For instance, the company had established a clear intellectual property rights (IPR) policy that it never entered into a contract with an external partner without agreeing on IPR issues in advance. This policy had resulted in impatient customers at times, but NKT Flexibles found the benefit of securing IPR extremely important. Furthermore, it focused intensively on building trust-based relationships with its external partners, as one of the key lessons from its many years of sourcing was the importance of strong, solid, and honest relationships with sourcing partners. A reliable relationship with the external partners was viewed as a primary premise for the sourcing of innovation projects, although once that prerequisite was fulfilled, it could be difficult to determine which partner should be responsible for which aspects of the partnership. In some cases, the sourcing firm did not have the necessary equipment, and huge investments were required from both the sourcing company and NKT Flexibles. In this regard, choosing to partner with the wrong company could be disastrous.

The sourcing strategy not only prompted changes and restructuring on the partner level – a number of internal initiatives were also
promoted. An internal investigation of the innovation process showed
that NKT Flexibles was more creative than innovative. Many of the
creative initiatives emerging from within the organization never
reached the production stage because of a lack of structural support.
As a consequence, the company established an Innovation Board with
the purpose of facilitating the process of transforming creativity into
actual innovation. The Innovation Board screened and appraised new
ideas for development, and prepared business cases for the steering
committee. The Innovation Board represented all areas of the company
and provided it with a holistic approach to incoming initiatives.

STAKEHOLDER ROLES IN THE INNOVATION STRATEGY

NKT Flexibles collaborated with different stakeholders in its innovation strategy, including universities, suppliers, and customers. The
stakeholders were involved in the innovation of the company's solutions and products, all of which were supplements to or variations on
the core product – the flexible pipe. These products included sensors,
valves, end-fittings, and special material solutions for extreme operational conditions. This arrangement ensured that the architectural
knowledge stayed within NKT Flexibles, but those supplements or
variations that the company did not have the competence and/or
technology to produce were outsourced. At times, this was nothing
more than a matter of adapting existing technology to the specific
context of flexible pipe systems (as with the type of valve for deepwater
applications). At other times, the development of a brand new technology was required (such as utilizing new fiber-reinforced material
based upon carbon fibers). The innovation funnel of NKT Flexibles is
shown in Figure 8.2.

Universities

NKT Flexibles's collaboration with universities was "more in the area
of new ideas," but rested on certain premises. For instance, the

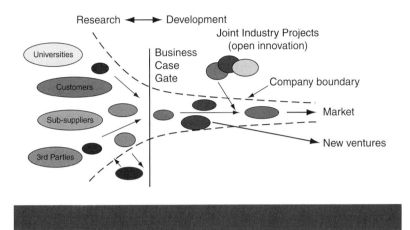

Source: Niels Rishøj, the 2009 European Outsourcing Summit, IAOP, 2009

FIGURE 8.2 NKT Flexibles's innovation-to-market funnel

company sent scouts to different conferences to seek out new ideas that might become useful. In addition, it invested in university projects in cases where a university could develop an idea into a new, useful technology. However, doing so was risky, as the university might never develop anything the company would find useful. In other words, although cooperation with universities might have provided it with access to the newest ideas and research, there was also a risk that such investments could have limited returns.

Despite the risk, NKT Flexibles cooperated with different universities on a number of different projects. Within deepwater development, its joint R&D activities with the universities focused on how to develop a deepwater pipe solution from scratch. Within the field of pipe structure optimization, it outsourced one R&D project to a university through the funding of a PhD scholarship.

In addition, NKT Flexibles cooperated with universities on improving material performance and in the area of monitoring pipes using optical fiber technology. In fact, the concept of gas monitoring of

Optical Gas Monitoring System Enters Test Stage

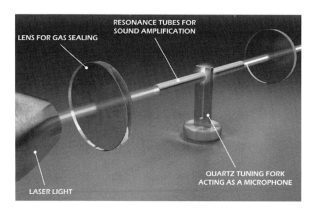

and continuously. Annulus gas monitoring is highly relevant for flexible pipes operational performance during design life period of the exceeding 20 years.

The small and robust sensing unit only needs a fiber-optical connection to work, making it ideal for deployment in explosion-hazard areas. The use of esonance quartz tuning fork makes the system immune to external noise and still very sensitive. Preliminary tests have shown accuracies of 2.2 ppm for H2S, 28 ppm for CO2 and 0.35 ppm for CH4 at sampling times of less than one minute. These accuracies are expected to improve as the system is tested and optimised.

NKT Flexibles is proud to announce the next phase in the development of our Optical Monitoring System (OMS), which already includes strain and temperature monitoring. It is the highly accurate real-time measurement of annulus gas concentrations, covering H2S, CO2 and CH4 in the first prototype.

The development is conducted in cooperation with the Laser Science Group at Rice University in Houston. The group has previously developed highly sensitive optical

gas sensors for use as early fire warning on the International Space Station. The patented sensing technique is called QEPAS (Quartz-Enhanced Photoacoustic Absorption Spectroscopy). It is basically the use of laser light to produce soundwaves in the gas, which are then collected with a quartz tuning fork for a highly accurate measure of all gas concentrations. The technique is superior to traditional gas sampling in that all gases constituents are measured simultaneously

Laboratory testing will continue into the spring of 2009, after which a commercial prototype will be built and tested on an oil platform. The finished product can also be retrofitted to any external piping connected to the annulus vent valve of an existing pipe.

The system is expected to be commercially available in late 2009. The results of the lab testing will be presented at OTC in technical session 312: 'Advances in Flexible Riser Technology' on Tuesday the 5th of May at 10.36 am.

Source: Flexpress April, 2009 – www.nktflexibles.com
FIGURE 8.3 Flexpress optical gas monitoring system

pipes using optical fibers came from a university context. Over time, the idea was developed into a joint project with the Laser Science Group at Rice University in Houston (Figure 8.3). NKT Flexibles signed a contract for a two-year R&D project including theoretical analysis, prototype design, and prototype testing.

Customers

Through its involvement with several customers, NKT Flexibles was able to develop another method of product innovation. The company practiced this type of open innovation with great success. For example, it worked closely with the Brazilian oil company Petrobras. The two companies had a joint R&D project on deepwater innovation. Rishøj referred to this project, stating: "They have plenty of their own ideas, which they share with us like brand new ways to do things within deepwater oil/gas production. Then we must go back and see if we can develop a flexible pipe solution to their problem, one way or another, and make it work in collaboration with Petrobras." In that case, Petrobras sourced assignments to NKT Flexibles – an example of how the open innovation could work in reverse. Both companies benefitted, as there was both an exchange of knowledge and the delivery of a concrete project.

Another example was an extension of the university innovation method. NKT Flexibles participated in a joint industry project (JIP) with other oil companies and firms with know-how in sensor technology in order to further develop the optical fibers that would meet the requirements for their use in flexible pipes. This JIP was based on a three-year contract and included theoretical analysis, the design and establishment of new processes, the manufacture of full-scale flexible pipes, full-scale verification testing, and final consolidation. This was therefore a more complex and resource-demanding project than the university projects, although it was dependent on the innovation undertaken by the universities.

Suppliers

The third innovation method used by NKT Flexibles was based on cooperation with its suppliers. This method had different angles, one of which was to assist in educating the supplier in the specific production requirements. In some cases, the supplier did not have the knowledge or the competencies needed to produce a specific part for a flexible pipe, but it might have the equipment or the capacity. NKT Flexibles would then help its partner acquire the missing knowledge and/or competencies through either knowledge transfers or financial support. As Rishøj stated, "we are the ones who have qualified this supplier to be able to deliver the product we need." In this manner, the company's relationship with its suppliers gained a more strategic character. Suppliers are being developed into strategic partners, and the character of the relationship is continuously being expanded and becoming more complex.

However, the experience of working with suppliers on a strategic R&D level resulted in the delineation of some factors that had to be considered before entering into a project. In an extreme case, a supplier showed no interest in properly developing a product it had agreed to produce for NKT Flexibles, and once the production had begun, NKT Flexibles found the quality of the product to be below its standards. However, no other suppliers were readily available and, given its promise to its customers to deliver only top-quality products, NKT Flexibles found itself in a dilemma. The product the supplier offered was not good enough, but there were no alternatives. Fortunately, some of the supplier's employees could see the potential in delivering the product at the required quality level, so they founded their own company in order to do so. The establishment of the new company was realized with the financial support of NKT Flexibles based on a promise from it to buy a certain amount of the product. Subsequently, the original supplier realized its mistake, but by then it was too late. Instead, NKT Flexibles proceeded to build a very strong relationship with the new company.

Overall, NKT Flexibles's cooperation with many of its suppliers was strategic. "Those we build a partnership with we intend to work closely with for say ten years or more, not least because we invest many resources in lifting them to the level we need them at," said Rishøj. One could say that the strategic considerations behind the different innovation methods were based on a gradual innovation process: While the universities were focused on the new technologies in the early development stages, the customers and suppliers were focused on more specific projects with the aim of developing a final product.

An important decision

Still sitting at his desk, Niels Rishøj was indecisive. On the one hand, the previous strategy had paid off – he was pleased with the pace of innovation both in-house and among the company's partners. On the other hand, he had had to work hard to maintain this level of success, and the increasing competition and globalization made it even harder. He knew that it was crucial to keep NKT Flexibles in its position as the most innovative and high-quality performer in its field. The question was how to do so.

In one way, strategic open innovation could be viewed as risk management in the sense that suppliers set their goals as a continuation of the NKT Flexibles strategy. This meant that NKT Flexibles could, almost automatically, meet its innovation goals in cooperation with its suppliers.

At the same time, however, open innovation and outsourcing were risky. Suppliers might lose momentum, fail to prioritize NKT Flexibles, or deliver in time. In addition, suppliers might not assign the same level of importance to innovation activities as NKT Flexibles. To deal with these dilemmas, Rishøj was required to allocate a considerable amount of resources to meetings, sparring, monitoring, and administration.

A third problem was the issue of communication. When dealing with a complex, unique product, communication was extremely important. However, language problems were frequent and prolonged the process in certain cases.

Therefore, Rishøj had several options to consider. He had three good but different open innovation methods. He had an opportunity to insource or to outsource. He knew the risks and benefits of all of his possible choices. The central question was: What kind of innovation mix should he suggest?

NKT FLEXIBLES: SUMMARY AND QUESTIONS FOR DISCUSSION

NKT Flexibles is a spin-off of a Danish conglomerate that has become a significant player in the world market for flexible pipe systems. The customers are mainly found in the oil and gas industry (for example, Statoil, Petrobas, etc.).

The case study of NKT Flexibles concerns a relatively small firm with limited resources for innovation, at least compared to its much larger competitors. However, despite its scarce resources, it has still managed to be very innovative and stay technologically ahead of its larger competitors. In fact, NKT Flexibles was the leading company in the world on advanced flexible pipe systems adapted to specific customer needs.

This is partly due to the company's strong focus on a narrow product niche that allows it to specialize and excel in its niche and partly due to innovations in its organizational setup. It is well aware that it will not able to generate the needed knowledge in all the technology areas it draws on, so instead it has developed a sophisticated model for collaborating with external partners including universities, suppliers, and customers. In doing so, it is largely building and orchestrating a network of partners where it has been very successful in tapping into new ideas and innovations generated in this partnership (as also indicated by the company's high EBITDA in the last couple of years).

This model provides NKT Flexibles with access to more knowledge than it would ever be able to generate itself. However, this collaborative model also comes at a cost, as the company has less control over the knowledge generation itself. It basically becomes much more dependent on its collaborators, and if it expected openness from its partners, the partners would expect the same from it. All in all it had to design the collaborative partnership in a fashion that would ensure that both parties gained something, while still minimizing the risks, for example, of knowledge leakage. As such, the case facilitates discussion of the following issues:

1. The collaborative strategy seems to have been beneficial for NKT Flexibles.
   a. What are the exact advantages of the collaborative strategy in R&D?
   b. Why could NKT Flexibles not just undertake all R&D in-house?
   c. What is the reaction among employees if R&D tasks are outsourced?
   d. How can the company appropriate value from these collaborative partnerships?
2. However, the strategy comes with some costs.
   a. What are these costs?
   b. What can NKT Flexibles do in order to minimize the risks?
   c. How can the company protect its knowledge?
3. In order to make the partnership viable in the long run, both parties needed to benefit from it.
   a. How can partnerships be set up so that both partners gain from the collaboration?
4. Not all partners are equal. It might be that certain partners are better for certain types of knowledge, etc.
   a. What type of knowledge can best be tapping into among: 1) universities, 2) customers, and 3) suppliers?
   b. What are the advantages and disadvantages of collaborating with these types of partners?

ADDITIONAL SOURCES IN RELATION TO NKT FLEXIBLES

www.nktflexibles.com/en

9   Concluding reflections: Innovating organization and management to stay competitive

"It is not the strongest species that survives. Not the most intelligent, it is the one that is most adaptable to change."

Charles Darwin

In a theory that is today referred to as "survival of the fittest," Charles Darwin presented his view of competition among different species. A similar theory can be applied to competition among firms. It is not necessarily those firms that are largest or have the most resources that do best, but rather those that are smartest, those that see the new opportunities, and those that develop new ways of doing business. What Darwin called "adaption to change" is similar to what we, in the context of competition among modern firms, denote as "management innovation." Management innovation is about finding new, smarter, and more efficient ways of organizing activities in firms. Often, changes in the firm's environment, such as the introduction of new technologies or consumer trends, create opportunities for management innovation. For example, the Internet has paved the way for many management innovations, like e-business and open source communities. In general, the most successful firms will be those that discover and seize new opportunities and then succeed in turning them into management innovations.

While technical innovation is about developing products and production processes, *management innovation* is defined as "the implementation of new management practices, processes and structures that represent a significant departure from current norms."[1] Note the elasticity of this definition: "Current norms" may be defined

---

[1] Birkinshaw and Mol, "How management innovation happens," 81.

at the level of the firm, the industry, or even the world. In the following, we think of management innovation in an equally pragmatic manner; thus, there is no pretension that what we here call management innovation is necessarily something that is new to the world. The key point is that while technical innovations aim at creating new activities (products or production processes), management innovations aim to organize activities in new ways in order to increase the value that firms can create and appropriate. As outlined in the first two chapters, we think of management innovations as encompassing the following aspects:

- new ways of configuring and coordinating the division of labor;
- new ways of rewarding employees;
- new ways of allocating authority;
- new ways of measuring input and output performance;
- new standard operating procedures;
- new ways of involving stakeholders; and
- new methods of global governance.

Basically, a management innovation is a new and better way of organizing, controlling, coordinating, and facilitating existing activities in the firm, explicitly implemented by management to increase value creation and appropriation, and perhaps to a confer competitive advantage on the firm.

The six Danish case studies in this book have focused on investigating the context of *management innovations* and how such innovations have unfolded in each company, and more broadly how these companies leverage organizational design and management practices to build strategic resources in the pursuit of competitive advantages. In an attempt to pull the various ideas and experiences together in this concluding chapter, we mainly discuss and reflect on those themes and aspects that emerge *across* the six cases.

The cases portrayed herein deviate to a great extent in a number of ways, for example, in terms of industries, markets, and ownership structures. Some of the more noticeable differences are listed in Table 9.1.

Table 9.1 *Basic characteristics of the six case companies*

Case company	Chr. Hansen	Coloplast	IC Companys	LEGO	NKT Flexibles	Vestas
Industry	Industrial enzymes	Ostomy and urology	Textiles	Toys	Flexible pipes	Wind turbines
Revenue (DKK million in 2007)	1,695	8,042	3,354	8,027	1,237	4,861
Employees in 2007	2,507	7,063	1,489	5,388	474	13,820
Market	B2B	B2C	B2C	B2C	B2B	B2B
Ownership	Capital foundation	Family	Family	Family	Conglomerate	Dispersed
Listed on stock exchange	No	Yes	Yes	No	No	Yes

Despite the clear differences among the six case companies, they all explicitly treat their organization and management systems as key strategic resources. In other words, they all take the design of the organization and its management practices very seriously indeed, recognizing that organization and management practice can be important sources of competitive advantage in their own right. Therefore, they strive to establish and maintain competitive advantages by means of improving management practices and organizational designs. The individual cases represent different manifestations of organizational arrangements and management processes that are certainly new to the firms involved and perhaps go beyond this to constitute new organizational forms and business models. However, the cases also reveal important and common features of management innovations across the cases. Rather than focus on how management innovation is handled in each individual case, this chapter focuses on those features of management innovation that appear across the cases. Therefore, the first section of this chapter, a) juxtaposes and maps the case companies on two dimensions: The scope and radicalism of the involved changes in organizational design and managerial practices, and b) discusses some of these basic dimensions as displayed across the case companies.

A distinction is commonly made in management theory among strategy, organization, and HRM in the firm. Based on this distinction, we have sought out some of the key changes applied across the six case companies in their efforts to implement new management practices and organizational designs. In this respect, the second section of this chapter categorizes the key features that are applied by the case companies when conducting changes in organizational designs and management processes.

In the third section, we consider the conditions or contextual settings under which changes in organization and management take place. Is it, for example, possible to point to internal or external contingencies that are likely to shape or determine novel transformations in organizational and management practices? Do such constituents increase or decrease the likelihood of successfully orchestrating such management innovations, i.e., the way that firms appropriate value from them and eventually turn them into competitive advantage?

To implement novel organization and management practices, and eventually gain and maintain a competitive advantage is a complex and uncertain process. There is no universal template upon which companies can rely. In fact, companies that challenge internal conventions and dogma in their search for novel organization and management practices often face a number of dilemmas, conflicts, or trade-offs. Therefore, the fourth section of this chapter presents and elaborates on dilemmas and key problem areas with reference to the case studies. The section reminds us of some of the process-related challenges firms face in orchestrating organizational and management changes, which may be relevant when the case studies are used in a classroom setting.

TWO BASIC DIMENSIONS OF MANAGEMENT INNOVATIONS

In the broader innovation literature it is common to distinguish between two basic dimensions of innovations, namely, the depth and breadth of innovations. The same typology can be applied for management innovations where the degree of depth is captured as the extent to which organizational and management practices/processes were fundamentally redefined as part of the change, and the degree of breadth as to the scope of the management innovation in question. This typology highlights that the scope and newness of the organizational changes can vary substantially from very radical changes that cut across many functions in the company (like the M-form in GM) or less radical changes that affect one or a few functions (like new incentive systems for managers). The six case companies can be categorized in terms of these two dimensions. In Figure 9.1, the specific positioning of each case company is based on our analysis of the case and not the company's own perception of the depth and breadth of the management innovation. Therefore, even if employees regard a given change in an organization as highly radical, it may build upon existing ways of doing business.

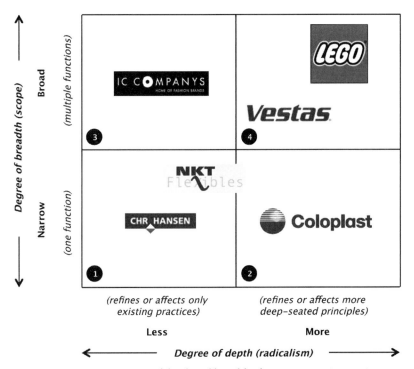

FIGURE 9.1 Degree of depth and breadth of management innovations

Quadrant 1 contains management innovations that primarily affect one or only a few organizational functions. These innovations are less radical, indicating a change of a relatively incremental nature in mainly one function. These kinds of transformations rarely alter fundamental principles and beliefs. The ingredient provider Chr. Hansen exemplifies such a change in management practice. The more explicit focus on employee performance (i.e., performance appraisals, assessments, and bonus systems) described in the case was aimed at infusing the organization with a stronger sense of account-ability and transparency. Although these changes were set in motion by the private equity fund PAI Partners, they were anchored and orchestrated by the HR function, which had been given much higher priority and greater power. The Chr. Hansen case also illustrates the aforementioned differences between the depth of change and employees' actual perception of these transformations. To management, a stronger, more transparent alignment between company goals and individual performance was central to building a high-performing culture. Goals were refined in the sense that they were broken down, even on lower organizational levels, and follow-up structures were defined and implemented all the way down to the level of the individual employee. Some employees, however, viewed these changes to "how we do business here" as negative and drastic, which ultimately led to the resignation of a number of them.

Quadrant 2 indicates management innovations that may not involve many organizational functions but that challenge and affect some deeply rooted management and organization principles. The medical device manufacturer and marketer Coloplast serves as an example of this kind of organizational change. As part of a global restructuring effort, the company worked to expand its R&D to include external innovation environments and to adopt, in some instances, a more radical approach to innovation. End-users had traditionally been instrumental in the development and design of new products. However, these user-driven R&D processes in most cases led to only incremental improvements rather than breakthrough ideas. Therefore, through its organizational transformation, Coloplast aimed to keep itself in close contact with internal and external innovation environments in order to better embrace radical innovation efforts. Rather than relying solely on internal R&D capabilities, a specialized external R&D function was developed to handle all open innovation activities, including technology scouting and partnerships. This function was designed to strengthen Coloplast's ability to identify, understand, and tap into available external knowledge. NKT Flexibles, which is placed on the borderline between quadrants 1 and 2, has experimented with open innovation which they are taking to the extreme in very open and sophisticated models for collaboration with external counterparts like universities, suppliers, and key customers.

Quadrant 3 represents a change in organization and management practices that covers multiple functional areas but has less depth. The case of IC Companys may exemplify this quadrant. The implementation of a brand-driven organization structured around individual brands in separate business units, coupled with support functions on the corporate level, can be seen as an attempt to strike a balance between external diversification (through the development of different brands) and the realization of economies of scale (through internal standardization and the pooling of back-office activities in a shared platform). The organizational reshuffle affected a number of functions because the internal division of activities was reorganized but the changes required limited behavioral change among employees.

Finally, *quadrant 4* exemplifies management innovations that affect multiple functions and challenges, and alter underlying beliefs and business principles. The toymaker the LEGO Group went through a deep-seated organizational overhaul that signaled a complete shift to a network-oriented business model with permeable boundaries and disintegrated value chain activities that spanned nearly all functional areas. This shift required substantial behavioral change on the part of its employees. The wind turbine maker Vestas Wind Systems represents a similar, although slightly less radical, change in organization and management processes. Following massive investments in global expansion (new production and R&D sites, headcount increases, etc.), the company needed to align employee and stakeholder interests globally. By applying governmental principles and rhetoric to avoid misunderstandings (such as the Vestas Government, the company constitution, etc.) and defining a series of constitution-enabling projects (which denoted the strategy execution method), the company's CEO wanted to instill and root the image of Vestas as a high-tech, fast-moving company among stakeholders and employees as opposed to a "traditional" industrial company.

As shown in Figure 9.1, the definition and implementation of novel approaches to organizational design and management practices does not necessarily involve all corporate functions or fundamentally alter underlying principles for the conduct of business. In fact, management innovations may take many shapes and forms, even within each polar position in the matrix (Figure 9.1), as demonstrated by the cases in this book. The typology improves our understanding of the fundamental dimensions along which management innovations may vary.

KEY CHANGES IN THE CASE COMPANIES

As we have seen, the cases presented here vary in many respects, including the scope and radicalism of the new organization and management principles and paradigms. It is also apparent from the case description that the management innovations have a very systemic character in the sense that changes to the organizational structure often go together with changes in HR, communication, etc., so the management innovation usually affects a larger part of the organization and not just a small corner of it. The systemic nature of management innovations is best illustrated in the LEGO Group and Vestas cases, which also implemented the most radical changes. However, a number of structural commonalities are still identifiable across the case studies, which we discuss in this section.

A distinction is commonly made in management theory between strategy, organization, and HRM in the firm. This distinction reflects the differing natures of strategy, organization, and HRM, and also highlights their links to different levels of the company – strategy is primarily defined on the management level, while organization refers to issues of delegation, departmentalization, and division of labor, and HRM includes different practices that target individual employees.

In the cases presented here, management innovations include changes in strategy (goal-setting), as well as changes in organization (organizational structures and delegation) and HRM (people management, incentive structures, and communications). The changes in strategy, organization, and HRM are not equally important in all six cases but, in all cases, the management innovations touch upon all three areas. In that sense, one can refer to the systemic nature of the management innovations in the case companies, as they are not isolated to only strategy, organization, or HRM, but typically include changes in all areas.

Table 9.2 presents these changes for the six case companies. The overall structure follows the distinction among strategy, organization, and HRM, but the key features are further disaggregated within these areas, so that *strategy* captures goal-setting and follow-up processes, *organization* is separated into organizational structure and delegation, and *HRM* is divided into people management, incentive structure, and communications. The disaggregation is based on careful analysis of the cases and identification of the important features of the various changes.

It seems clear that not all of the changes in organization design and management practices that have been documented in the cases are proper management innovations. Much of what we see is a result of the companies making organizational changes that reflect what they believe are best practices. This is well described by a manager at Coloplast, who emphasized: "Most of what we do, probably 80 percent, is implementing best practice, and much of this is based on ideas gained from consulting firms. But for a small part, we deviate from others and experiment with new ways of organizing our activities" (John Raabo Nielsen, Senior Vice-President, Global R&D, Coloplast). Therefore, distinct management innovations are to be found in the remaining 20 percent of changes, where the company deviates from the processes of other companies (recognized best practices) and searches for new ways of doing business.

In the following, we discuss the findings for each of these features. We focus on some of the more important and intriguing findings – areas in which the case companies deviate from each other. These findings are highlighted in gray in Table 9.2.

Goal-setting and the follow-up process

All six companies have implemented changes in their goal-setting and follow-up processes. They have all worked on clarifying exact goals (e.g., in terms of profitability and growth) and have translated them

Table 9.2 *Key features and structural commonalities in the case studies*

	LEGO Group	Chr. Hansen	Coloplast	IC Companys	NKT Flexibles	Vestas
			STRATEGY			
Goal-setting and follow-up processes	– Before: Owners unclear of goals; now: Profitability – Clearly defined goals	– Clear goals are set for revenue, EBITA, and working capital – Monthly business review process – Monthly email on financial performance to top 100 managers	– Growth is the main goal – "The products need to be developed at a much higher pace" (CCO Lars Rasmussen) – Regular assessment of results – Standardization of financial reporting and implementation of KPIs	– Growth: 15%; EBIT: 15% – Develop customer orientation in brands – Meeting with brand directors 5–6 times per year – Developing KPIs and standardized reporting	– Many goals in terms of R&D and innovation	– Profitability more important than growth – High ambitions: "The will to win," "No. 1 in Modern Energy," and "Failure is not an option" – Global market share goal of 35% – Standardized reporting (four pages)

ORGANIZATION

Organizational structure	– Outsourcing and offshoring to optimize organization; from vertical integration to network structure – Opening up the company in relation to fans, customers, suppliers, etc. – Opening up toward global suppliers	– Creating a product-oriented organization and a global sales division; pursuing product excellence – New management team	– From divisional to functional organization – Expand and integrate global network of subsidiaries/innovation partners – More outsourcing	– Multibrand structure based on shared platform	– Strong internal R&D organization in order to match external partners	– Clear management structure with presidents who each have a well-defined area of responsibility – Transparency, communication, and delegation the key parameters in organizational structure – State-of-affairs meetings with top managers every Wednesday ("they know everything")
Delegation		– Project and team organization – High level of task responsibility – Common ground topped with individual delegation	– Empowerment of the organization – De-bureaucratization – More delegation of mandates to subsidiaries	– Substantial delegation of task responsibility to brands ("live the brand") – Each brand runs as an independent company with bottom-line responsibility	– Openness toward external partners – Substantial delegation to project teams internally	– Substantial delegation – Whistleblower function to identify irregularities

Table 9.2 (cont.)

	LEGO Group	Chr. Hansen	Coloplast	IC Companys	NKT Flexibles	Vestas
			HRM			
People management	– Upgrading HR	– Significant upgrading of HRM as a strategic tool – Individual development related to business goals – Building of a performance culture – Focus on leadership	– Standardization in R&D (lean) versus creativity – Leadership training – Establishment of commercial excellence function to professionalize sales, marketing, and management	– Building an international HR organization and running four academies for internal training (leaders, sales, retails, and brands) – HR as a key strategic focus area	– Focus on HR and explaining the collaboration strategy to all employees	– Strong focus on and upgrading of people and culture; People & Culture unit – Strong focus on internal cohesiveness: One Vestas – Promoting a culture with more emphasis on innovation – Recruit diverse profiles
Incentive structure	– Introducing a performance-based culture (5–30% of salary)	– Increasing interest-bearing debt – Managers urged/required to invest own money in firm	– Managers must apply for own jobs	– Brand directors measured on performance – Performance-based bonuses	– Incentives built into partnership contracts	– Bonus system mainly based on company performance
Communication	– Weekly newsletter and CEO blog – More interaction with fans and customers	– Monthly email to all employees – Frequent visits to foreign subsidiaries	– Improving informal communication through new	– Improvement of IT system as a way to communicate	– Extensive communication given the small size of the company	– Upgrading of internal communication, such as CEO webcast

- Very focused on internal communication
- "Without Teflon" communication

- Breakdown of local "kingdoms"

organizational structure
- Improving formal communication through standardization

- Rethinking marketing strategies – more "bang for the buck"

- Heavy external communication through global media
- Focus on getting to influential decision makers; establishment of governmental relations department

into slogans (such "3 times 15 in 2015" – Vestas) that are easy to communicate internally and externally. Furthermore, the follow-up process has been a focus area, where the trend has been to simplify and standardize reporting in a few KPIs that can be easily compared across departments and over time. Fast and standardized reporting makes benchmarking across the company much easier. All of the companies have implemented these kinds of changes, but Chr. Hansen and Vestas stand out as those that have been most radical in terms of changing their goal-setting and follow-up processes, as indicated in Table 9.2.

Chr. Hansen's change of ownership through its takeover by the capital foundation PAI Partners infused the company with a new culture that was clearly focused on goal-setting and accountability on all levels. This was achieved through the implementation of monthly result reviews (KPIs) and benchmarking of all units in the company, which involved communication with the top 100 managers. Vestas made its reporting system and follow-up process equally transparent by shortening the performance reports from each function and department to a maximum of four pages that centered on a few KPIs, which enabled internal benchmarking. However, the company went further in formulating simple slogans like "The Will to Win" and "No. 1 in Modern Energy," slogans that capture the company's ambitious goals. These slogans are heavily used in internal communications and in external communications, where the global media is the main target for financial presentations. Chr. Hansen has innovated in terms of the way in which goals and accountability are rolled out across the entire organization, while Vestas has innovated in terms of communicating goals internally and externally.

Organizational structure

All six companies have made changes to their organizational structure; however, the LEGO Group and Vestas have gone much further than the other companies in terms of changing their organizational structures.

The LEGO Group has been undergoing a dramatic transition in which the underlying logic of the change has been to return to the company's "old" core values while also opening up toward external counterparts to make the boundaries of the firm more permeable. As a result of this process, fans, key customers, and suppliers are taken much more seriously as a true source of new ideas and are invited to become partners in some of the firm's key activities, notably product development and design. In particular, the enormous energy and creativity of LEGO fans is harnessed by inviting them to join in the development and design of future LEGO products.

The changes in Vestas seem less dramatic and more of a symbolic nature, as they are posted in the form of a "governmental" rhetoric. However, they are still significant and remarkable. In Vestas, the CEO and CFO are presidents, and each of the twelve functions is managed by a minister. The Vestas Government consists of the two presidents and the twelve ministers, who meet every Wednesday for a state-of-affairs meeting. All this is written out in the Vestas Constitution. By encompassing management practices in this government rhetoric, Vestas signals that it has implemented a decision-oriented management structure that enables collective decision making – and that the company has a powerful team that takes management decisions seriously.

Delegation

Empowering organizations and delegating decision authority/rights to those that have the right knowledge is one set of changes undertaken in most companies. However, none of the companies have struggled as much with issue as IC Companys. For IC Companys, the challenge has been to strike a balance between its multibrand structure and its shared platform. In the eyes of the customer, the eleven brands of IC Companys must appear to be clearly distinct in order avoid cannibalization. This requires substantial delegation of task responsibility to the designers for each brand, so that they can "live the brand" and create distinct brands. On the other hand, the platform shared by all of the brands includes back-office activities, like the supply chain, distribution, marketing, and IT, all of which are necessary to make IC Companys profitable. In fact, the company might only be able to achieve profitability if it succeeds in exploiting economies of scale in its back-office activities. It has experimented extensively with its organizational design in order to strike the right balance among these conflicting interests.

In terms of the delegating responsibility, the key question is how much responsibility brand designers should have. Should they have influence over the choice of suppliers for their particular brand (the actual workroom) or should that be optimized for all brands? Another related issue is the selection of activities to be offered using the shared platform. For example, should marketing be brand-specific or can it be handled across brands simultaneously? Another issue along the same lines is the question of internal payments for the services offered on the shared platform. Should all brands pay the same amount for the shared platform although their use of the offered services might differ significantly? Clearly, striking the right balance between the multibrand structure and the shared platform requires consideration of many organizational design issues – IC Companys has experimented with different solutions over the years to fine-tune its organizational setup.

The delegation issue is also a key part of the management innovation in the case of NKT Flexibles, but here it is more in relation to the external counterparts. Over the years, the company has gradually gone further and further in delegation, openness, and empowerment of external collaborators. It has step-by-step learned how to set up more sophisticated partnerships that benefit all the involved partners and still minimize the risks of such issues as knowledge leakage.

People management

All of the case companies are upgrading their people management skills and all intend to build a stronger performance culture among employees. This trend is best exemplified by Chr. Hansen with its introduction of PDIs as a tool for strengthening employee competences, and for maintaining the focus on the development and performance of individual employees. A similar development has taken place in Vestas, where the HRM function has been renamed People & Culture – as people and culture is what it is all about. Vestas is also applying various measures to promote diversity (such as the recruitment of diverse profiles) and create a culture with more emphasis on innovation (through, for example, internal competitions on innovation).

Coloplast is struggling with its need to implement lean principles of standardization throughout the company, while maintaining creativity and motivation among its R&D employees. How can it reap the benefits of standardization in R&D without lowering creativity? Resolving these issues may result in a management innovation that could provide the firm with additional competitive advantages.

Incentive structure

Changes in the incentive structure are also evident in all six cases in terms of a stronger link between performance and payment. The most radical change is seen in Chr. Hansen, which now urges managers to invest in the company in order to align the interest of owners and managers. In the other companies, the share of remuneration that depends on individual or team (Vestas) performance has been increased. Coloplast took another route in the sense that it established a mechanism requiring all managers to apply for their own jobs, which allowed the company to reshuffle the organization and pick the best-performing managers for different tasks.

Communication

The importance of communication cannot be exaggerated – all case companies have significantly increased the amount of attention paid to internal and external communication. This requires the use of professional means of communication, the delivery of open and honest information, and an increase in the amount of communication, for example, in weekly or monthly emails or newsletters. Most of the communication is internal and is aimed at all employees in the global organization. However, external communication is also expanding through more open, sincere communication with external stakeholders. LEGO, for example, focuses on extensive, ongoing communication with LEGO fans who are organized into LEGO fan groups around the world. This extensive communication with LEGO fans involves many employees – even the CEO has set up channels for dialogs with fans. Vestas is more oriented toward the political sphere, where it has professionalized its communication and lobbying through such activities as the establishment of a department for government relations.

Internal and external communication is by far the most time-consuming task for CEOs. The use of the new information and communication technologies plays an important role, but the content and form of the communication have also been upgraded and professionalized in all companies.

THE CONTEXTUAL SETTING: CENTRAL TO MANAGEMENT INNOVATIONS

In reflective chapters such as this, it is tempting to examine antecedents that are instrumental in the formation of novel organizational and management practices. In such an exercise, there is inherent potential for intellectual sidetracking (or bias), which may lead to distorted descriptions of cause and effect relationships.[2] However, the purpose of such an exercise is to probe further into the situational setting that existed prior to an innovation in organization and management principles. For example, is it possible to point to internal or environmental aspects that might have had a triggering effect?

In terms of possible antecedents to management innovations in the case companies, it is clear that, in most cases, some kind of external pressure – whether from competition or boards – created a sense of urgency to varying degrees. Consider the LEGO Group for a

---

[2] Philip Rosenweig, *The Halo Effect … and the Eight Other Business Delusions that Deceive Managers* (New York: Free Press, 2007).

moment. Prior to the thorough organizational overhaul and the sub-sequent change in the business model, the company reported accumu-lated losses of DKK 2.7 billion for 2003 and 2004. In other words, the company was destroying value to such an extent that dramatic changes were needed in order for the company to survive. With a strong man-date from the board, the company's CEO, Jørgen Vig Knudstorp, launched a *financial transformation plan* to stabilize the company. Only after the successful introduction of that financial transformation did the company have the necessary financial and organizational strength to undertake a deep-seated transformation of its management processes and practices – a transformation that aimed to redefine the boundaries of value chain activities and thereby illuminate a new organizational design.

The "burning platform" sense of urgency at IC Companys and Vestas Wind Systems, although less ominous than in the LEGO case, also helped to define new organization and management principles. The clothing retailer was struggling, as sales and profits had plum-meted from 2001 through 2004. Key shareholders were anxious to counteract this negative trend. They therefore installed a new manage-ment team, which defined a new strategic and organizational platform characterized by a clear division of labor. The new platform also attempted to deal with the Achilles heel of IC Companys– the lack of sufficient commercial attitudes among brand designers.

Despite its undisputed position as the world's largest wind tur-bine maker, Vestas's earning margins were small, operational prob-lems were a nagging concern, and its strategy lacked a clear direction. Moreover, the company's image was still permeated by views of wind energy as "the alternative" and "romanticism," views that were far from Vestas's perception of itself as a professional-driven, efficient, and innovative energy company. Vestas had, in other words, a need to redefine itself to realize its potential.

Chr. Hansen and Coloplast represent cases in which the "burn-ing platform motive" is less predominant. The triggering effect for Chr. Hansen was primarily the change from public to private equity ownership, which sparked a more explicit focus on performance and accountability at all levels. At Coloplast, the organization and management rearrangement grew out of internal discontent (executive management and the Board) with business development, and the failure to meet pre-defined revenue and earnings targets.

In sum, the antecedents in the case studies are largely related to some dissatisfaction with the status quo. This dissatisfaction provokes a sense of urgency and helps to initiate changes in or renewal of the organization and management practices and processes.

DILEMMAS, CONFLICTS, AND TRADE-OFFS IN IMPLEMENTING MANAGEMENT INNOVATIONS

Most organizational changes emerge out of dilemmas and conflicts, while trade-offs need to be dealt with in order to make any change more sustainable. In fact, management innovations often evolve as firms struggle with the dilemmas that they face. Table 9.3 lists some of the dilemmas facing the six case companies. For example, the LEGO Group is opening up for external stakeholders, and empowering fans and involving them in the development and design of new LEGO products. This process releases a wealth of ideas and creativity among LEGO fans, which has the potential to become an important source of product innovation. However, in order to exploit this potential, LEGO must shift the culture among its employees away from arrogance and the neglect of external competencies (the "not invented here" syndrome). The company also has to address vital issues, such as protecting the LEGO brand, handling IPR issues and setting deadlines, when collaborating with LEGO fans who are not employed by or in any other means contractually related to LEGO, but who are just extremely passionate about and emotionally connected to LEGO's products.

Another dilemma is the ever-present trade-off between the multiple brands and the shared platform in IC Companys. Where should the line be drawn between the brands and the shared platform, and what is the best mechanism for paying for services used through the

Table 9.3 *Key dilemmas and problem areas discussed in the case studies*

LEGO Group	Chr. Hansen	Coloplast	IC Companys	NKT Flexibles	Vestas Wind Systems
Organizational structure	**Goal-setting and clearly defined follow-up processes**	**Organizational structure**	**Organizational structure**	**Organizational structure**	**Organizational structure**
– Managing the increased complexity of "opening" the value chain (i.e., transaction costs, coordination issues, principal-agent issues, cultural issues, etc.)	– Managing a cultural shift from complacency to an explicit focus on human performance	– Adopting a more standardized (global scale) approach to sales, marketing, and R&D without compromising creativity	– Optimizing the division of labor (roles and responsibilities), and realizing synergies among brand units and the shared platform (primarily back-office functions)	– Handling openness toward external collaborators without running the risk of losing knowledge	– Handling and following high-growth scenarios without losing control of organization and finances
	Communication	– Expanding R&D to include external innovation environments and connecting	**People management**	**Incentive structure**	– Tackling financial problems
– Relocating and outsourcing production to	– Internally crafting and selling the message of private equity		– Balancing the employee mix	– Making collaboration beneficial for partners and still appropriate value for themselves	**People management**
					– Getting all employees in the outermost areas/

Table 9.3 (cont.)

LEGO Group	Chr. Hansen	Coloplast	IC Companys	NKT Flexibles	Vestas Wind Systems
offshore destinations – Including users in product development (i.e., changing roles and responsibilities, IPRs, etc.) – Bridging efforts within new business development (i.e., digitalization) with LEGO's	ownership and the objective – "Mentally" preparing the organization for an exit (i.e., maintain focus, momentum, energy levels, etc.) **Incentive structure** – Defining and creating the right incentives to ensure	these with internal R&D efforts while avoiding, for example, the "not invented here" syndrome – Adopting, in some instances, a more radical approach to innovation – Integrating strategic acquisitions into the organization	between commercial and creative skillsets (i.e., managers with the creative process and designers with commercial instincts) – Ensuring an adequate level of human capacity in each brand **Goal-setting and clearly defined**		parts of the company to buy into the self-image of proliferation, especially given the high level of complexity (i.e., globalization of production and R&D, increasing number of employees, etc.) **Communication** – Instilling and rooting the

core (and physical) products

People management

– Ensuring a clear focus on performance and execution (individual) without compromising internal collaboration (teams)

Communication

– Managing continuity while avoiding complacency (as dedication, motivation, and buy-in on the part of the employees

follow-up processes

– Ensuring that design resonates with commercial interest, i.e., a fact-based approach to design versus gut feelings

Delegation and communication

– Balancing brands' interest in developing own universes and subcultures, and corporate interests in image of Vestas as a high-tech, fast-moving company among stakeholders and employees as opposed to image as a "traditional" industrial company

– Changing the perception of wind energy to that of an economic and rational competitor to oil and gas

Table 9.3 (cont.)

LEGO Group	Chr. Hansen	Coloplast	IC Companys	NKT Flexibles	Vestas Wind Systems
opposed to change/crisis management)			maintaining unity – Avoiding potential power struggles among brands while ensuring best practices and knowledge sharing across brands		– Tackling current and past problem areas (turbine crashes and poor customer satisfaction) while communicating the message "No. 1 in Modern Energy"

shared platform? How can the company create the best conditions for creativity and innovation, and still encourage customer orientation and commercial skills among brand designers? A better solution to this dilemma would put IC Companys ahead of its competitors, which are struggling with similar dilemmas.

For Vestas, one main challenge is to change the perception of the company from its image as a traditional metal company that produces windmills to a modern, fast-moving, and innovative company that offers wind turbines that produce environmentally friendly energy. It is a major challenge to convince employees and external stakeholders of Vestas's new image, since the company's fundamental activities have not really changed significantly.

Coloplast is faced with the need to apply lean principles of standardization in R&D without compromising creativity. In addition, the company is seeking a new mechanism that will infuse its R&D activities with more groundbreaking ideas, as extensive interaction with users has mainly generated only incremental innovations.

The main dilemma for NKT Flexibles is how far it can go in collaboration with external partners. It cannot treat external partners entirely as if they were internal (e.g., it needs to have sorted out IPR issues up-front), but it can go very far in its collaboration even with some of its important R&D. But exactly how far it can go without getting its fingers burnt is the current dilemma.

Table 9.3 lists more dilemmas that are discussed in the six cases. These dilemmas are often the starting point for management innovations, as a management innovation itself might be a new way of dealing with such dilemmas.

Index